Writing
a
Thesis

Writing a Thesis

SUBSTANCE AND STYLE

R. Keith Van Wagenen
Arizona State University

PRENTICE HALL, Englewood Cliffs, New Jersey 07632

Library of Congress Cataloging-in-Publication Data

Van Wagenen, R. Keith.
    Writing a thesis : substance and style / R. Keith Van Wagenen.
        p.   cm.
    Includes bibliographical references.
    Includes index.
    ISBN 0-13-971086-8
    1. Dissertations, Academic.   I. Title.
    LB2369.V257   1990
    808'.02--dc20
                                                    90-36107
                                                        CIP

Editorial/production supervision
    and interior design: Serena Hoffman
Cover design: Carol Ceraldi
Manufacturing buyer: Robert Anderson

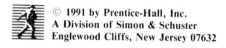

© 1991 by Prentice-Hall, Inc.
A Division of Simon & Schuster
Englewood Cliffs, New Jersey 07632

Printed in the United States of America
10   9   8   7

ISBN 0-13-971086-8

PRENTICE-HALL INTERNATIONAL (UK) LIMITED, *London*
PRENTICE-HALL OF AUSTRALIA PTY. LIMITED, *Sydney*
PRENTICE-HALL CANADA INC., *Toronto*
PRENTICE-HALL HISPANOAMERICANA, S.A., *Mexico*
PRENTICE-HALL OF INDIA PRIVATE LIMITED, *New Delhi*
PRENTICE-HALL OF JAPAN, INC., *Tokyo*
SIMON & SCHUSTER ASIA PTE. LTD., *Singapore*
EDITORA PRENTICE-HALL DO BRASIL, LTDA., *Rio de Janeiro*

To Linda, Nick, Kathy,
Stan, Cheri, Merilu, and Polly,
and to all those students of research writing
from whom I learned what should be
the content of this book

Contents

CHAPTER 3
How to Write a Research Introduction 33

CHAPTER 4
How to Write a Method Section   65

CHAPTER 5
How to Write a Results Section   73

Foreword

While serving on students' supervisory committees, I received proposals in which, even in first draft, students offered well-structured, well-reasoned, and answerable questions as the focus of their studies. That experience was strikingly different from others in which students did not explain their research problems or show how the anticipated results might cast light on a problem not then understood. I was curious about what accounted for the difference.

It turned out that almost all of the students whose proposals had caught my attention and who seemed well prepared for the research endeavor had taken Professor Van Wagenen's course "Expository Writing and Research Heuristics," or they had studied mimeographed versions of this book. During the several years in which Professor Van Wagenen allowed me to assign this manuscript-in-progress to students, I escaped countless hours of laborious explanation in trying to undo erroneous notions about what constitutes a research question and how to express that question in writing.

Students in the arts and sciences and professional schools will write more confidently—and certainly with greater satisfaction from their mentors—when they have mastered this book. In my personal library, *Writing a Thesis: Substance and Style* will be shelved next to that other invaluable resource, a style manual, in my case the *Publication Manual of the American Psychological Association*. Students will really value this book. Professors will enjoy it too, as a prime or supplementary text in their research courses.

Lee Meyerson
Regents' Professor
Arizona State University

Acknowledgments

For careful reading of early drafts and resulting changes in the manuscript, I'm grateful to colleagues Brendan Bartlett, Joy Burke, Garry Martin, Lee Meyerson, Ed Nelsen, and Howard Sullivan, and to the publisher's reviewers: Lawrence Herringer, California State University–Chico; Stephen N. Elliot, University of Wisconsin–Madison; Richard Elardo, The University of Iowa; Nancy G. Pollock, North Carolina State University; John M. McGuire, University of Central Florida; Garry L. Martin, St. Paul's College–University of Manitoba; and Richard F. Schmid, Concordia University.

Students and former students really helped; I hope they know how much I value that help. In particular are Susan Wilkinson, who assembled the various statistical examples in the results chapter and ran data to be sure they would be internally consistent; Roxie Covey and Frank Yekovich, who helped with early drafts of the style chapter, and Randall Russac, who allowed me to base an example proposal on his published research.

R. Keith Van Wagenen

Writing
a
Thesis

CHAPTER

1

About You as a Writer and This Book

PURPOSE OF THE BOOK

This book has a single purpose: to help you compose research documents—theses, dissertations, journal articles, and related writings. Its advice is given in detail. Each section explains what should be written and how to write it. Every effort was made to make these imperatives plain, bold, and clear. This book should be your friend. Groucho Marx once said, "Outside of a dog, a book is a man's best friend; inside of a dog, it's too dark to read." Read this book in the light, sitting in a hard chair, and giving it your full attention.

It's hard to get graduate research started, and harder yet to get it finished. You may have had little experience doing and reporting research, and you can hardly know how to perform such a complex task without first learning a lot about it. Chapter 2 tells you what steps to take before attempting a proposal, then how to write one. If you follow this advice, you can get started. The rest of the book will get you through a final report, one step at a time.

This book offers structure for all the research documents you must write. It tells you what should be in the difficult sections to write (for example, the introduction) and the order in which to write. Until you have had enough experience to know which expositional devices work and which do not, you will find comfort in ample structure. You want an easier task, and you also want effective content.

THE SORRY STATE OF RESEARCH WRITING

The writing in student research and even in research journals does not present a happy picture. This kind of writing is a demanding mental exercise for anyone, but for some of us, it's torture. There simply isn't enough training and practice in graduate school to help bright people think and express their thoughts in an organized and understandable way.

Woodford (1967), in the journal *Science,* addressed the topic "Sounder Thinking through Clearer Writing." The collective opinions of many editors speak through Woodford, who wrote:

> All are agreed that the articles in our journals—even the journals with the highest standards—are, by and large, poorly written. Some of the worst are produced by the kind of author who consciously pretends to a "scientific scholarly" style. He takes what should be lively, inspiring, and beautiful and, in an attempt to make it seem dignified, chokes it to death with stately abstract nouns; next, in the name of scientific impartiality, he fits it with a complete set of passive constructions to drain away any remaining life's blood or excitement; then he embalms the remains in molasses of polysyllable, wraps the corpse in an impenetrable veil of vogue words, and buries the stiff old mummy with much pomp and circumstance in the most distinguished journal that will take it. Considered either as a piece of scholarly work or as a vehicle of communication, the product is appalling. The question is, Does it matter?
>
> . . . Sometimes a skeptic will ask me, "Do you really think it's so important to improve scientific writing? We know it's usually a bit on the pompous side, but

once you get used to the conventions you can zip through it pretty easily and get to the author's meaning."

Personally, I *don't* find it so easy to zip through the pretentious constructions, and I think that one all too frequently arrives at a meaning that was not intended. But more telling than either of these reasons for concern is this: I have definite and clear-cut evidence that the scientific writing in our journals exerts a corrupting influence on young scientists—on their writing, their reading, and their thinking. (p. 743)

A RATIONALE: THE THINKING BEHIND RESEARCH

Very often students have the idea that writing a thesis is simply a matter of assembling their problem statements, methods, and analyzed data. They assume that research is simply an empirical act, untouched by their own rationales and analyses. They are unaware of the *craft* involved in writing a thesis. Even greater than their inadequacies of expression are their conceptual inadequacies. The ideal toward which we strive in doing research is to contribute convincing thought to our field of study. If an empirical contribution seems enough, look again at a dictionary definition of *empirical,* but don't miss part of the definition. The term implies *more* than observations of real phenomena. A definition that includes phrases like "dependent on observations only", or "without respect to theory or science," is charlatanism. Of course, *empirical* has certain positive connotations as well.

The thinking or rationale aspect of writing is the hardest part of research reporting. Woodford (1967) maintained that writing practice in class improves a writer's logic, and he argued that what is lacking in students' written copy is clear thought:

> But it is seldom pointed out that the very act of writing can help to clarify thinking. Put down woolly thoughts on paper, and their woolliness is immediately exposed. If students come to realize this, they will write willingly and frequently at all stages of their work, instead of relegating "writing up" to the very end and regarding it as a dreadful chore that has very little to do with their "real" work. (p. 744)

Pay special attention to this next point. It reveals the content most often missing in research reports. I have made this missing element central in Chapter 2, about writing a proposal, and Chapter 3, about writing an introduction:

> . . . these stylistic considerations only scratch the surface of what is really at fault in many scientific articles. I am appalled by the frequent publication of papers that describe most minutely what experiments were done, and how, but with no hint of why, or what they mean. Cast thy data upon the waters, the authors seem to think, and they will come back interpreted.
>
> If this approach to publication is to be successfully thwarted by a course on scientific writing, the course should *concentrate primarily on clarifying the students' thoughts about the purpose of a piece of research,* the conclusions that can justifiably be drawn, and the significance of those conclusions; matters of style are of subsidiary importance. (Woodford, 1967, p. 744; emphasis added)

A rationale is an explanation built around a research problem.   Moreover, a rationale should identify a problem and show what makes it problematic. Students find identifying and explaining their research problems to be the most difficult task facing them in writing a thesis. Again from Woodford:

> Students, with their recent results in mind, can often tell you what their *answers* are, but they are not always so sure of what the *question* was. Here is the first opportunity to test the hypothesis that writing clarifies thought. When they write down the questions asked and the answers obtained, students frequently come to see that the answers they have are to questions different from what they had thought. (p. 744, 745)

At the time Harry Harlow (1962) retired as editor of the *Journal of Comparative and Physiological Psychology,* he gave future manuscript writers some tongue-in-cheek advice about how to reveal their research problems:

> Although some psychologists write simple, straightforward introductions, this is commonly considered to be *declassé.* In the sophisticated or "striptease" technique you keep the problem a secret from the reader until the very last paragraph. Indeed, some very sophisticated authors keep the problem a secret forever. Since I am interested in readers as well as authors, I advise that readers always approach introduction sections using the Chinese technique—begin at the end and read backward. (editorial, p. 893)

Professor Harlow was right; the quickest way to understand is first to find out what is to be understood. When a research problem is presented first, before its basis or rationale, readers comprehend it more easily. Chapter 7, on writing style, begins by advocating that you should write the central idea first; other concepts then follow more easily.

YOUR MAJOR PROFESSOR AND SELF-IMPROVEMENT

It is unlikely that you will ever again receive the personal critical attention that a major professor will give to your intellectual development. Professors often identify with their students, hoping to put the best possible finish on them. My mentor acknowledged a large contribution from his mentor, and I must certainly acknowledge the same from mine. Under favorable conditions, the opportunity to learn and to form habits during graduate study is singular and remarkable. Fortunate is the student who sees it this way. Choose a major professor who will require good performance of you, not one who sets a low standard for his or her students.

Because writing research reports is a complex task, it always involves revisions.   You have substantive ideas to get across that require thinking and rethinking, revision after revision. It's natural for you to feel frustrated when you don't meet your own standard or someone else's. Such is the ordinary course of research reporting. Accept it; then turn your attention to learning to do it with greater ease.

CONTENT OF THIS BOOK

Research writing is above all else argumentative and persuasive.   When you write an understandable report, there is a close union between writing style and research logic. Elements of research logic are called *heuristic* matters. There are eight states in the United States with towns named Eureka, from the Greek for "I have found." These towns got their names when discoverers of mineral wealth shouted in their ecstacy, "Eureka!" *Heuristic* (to discover) and *eureka* originated from the same Greek word (*heureka*). In methods of research and philosophy of discovery, the word *heuristic* has come to refer to all the elements of strategy and logic investigators use to make scientific discoveries and convince others that they have indeed discovered something.

Heuristic concepts appear in what you write.   In this book, Chapters 2 through 6 tell what to include in a thesis proposal and in a thesis itself (introduction, method, results, and discussion). The content of these documents is heuristic; that is, the content is a subtle argument about search and discovery having to do with what can be believed about the phenomena studied.

The concept "What is a research problem?" is the key topic of Chapters 2 and 3. Chapter 2 tells how to write a thesis proposal, and Chapter 3, how to write an introduction. Chapter 3 should be read along with Chapter 2 because its content extends and elaborates the content of the preceding chapter.

Chapter 7 is about *exposition*—the style of writing found in research literature and textbooks. The guiding principle is: Complete and accurate information should be given away with the least expense to readers. This chapter is meant to improve your written expression.

USING THIS BOOK WITH A FORM AND STYLE MANUAL

The content of this book is different from that of a form or style manual. Form and style manuals include rules like those for putting a list in a series within a paragraph, or those for what can and cannot be abbreviated, or those for constructing tables and figures. Take these matters of form and style seriously; your graduate committee will.

Most fields of science and most professional organizations have form or style manuals for writers to use when submitting manuscripts to journals published by those organizations. You should have a copy of the manual recommended for your field of study. If your graduate school has a guide for writing theses and dissertations, get it before doing your research.

Before buying a manual, find out which one is used in your program of study. Many professional schools and colleges in business, education, nursing, and various disciplines of the social sciences use the *Publication Manual of the American Psychological Association*. Some of the most commonly used form and style manuals are:

Agriculture: American Society of Agronomy. (1984). *Publications handbook and style manual.* Madison, WI: American Society of Agronomy; Crop Science Society of America; Soil Science Society of America. 76 pages.

Biology: CBE Style Manual Committee. (1983). *CBE style manual* (5th ed., rev.). Bethesda, MD: Council of Biology Editors, Inc. 324 pages.

Chemistry: American Chemical Society. (1986). *The ACS style guide: A manual for authors and editors.* Washington, DC: American Chemical Society. 264 pages.

Education: National Education Association of the United States. (1966). *NEA style manual.* Washington, DC: Publications Division of the National Education Association. (Some education fields of study also use the *Publication Manual of the American Psychological Association.*) 76 pages.

Medicine: American Medical Association. (1976). *Stylebook/editorial manual of the AMA* (6th ed.). Acton, MA: Publishing Sciences Group. 161 pages.

Physics: American Institute of Physics. (1978). *Style manual for the publication of papers for journals published by the American Institute of Physics and its member societies* (3rd ed., rev.). New York: Publication Board of the American Institute of Physics. 56 pages.

Psychology and other social sciences: American Psychological Association. (1983). *Publication manual of the American Psychological Association* (3rd ed.). Washington, DC: Publications and Communications Board of the American Psychological Association. 208 pages.

This book is not intended to favor only one kind of research. The writer of any type of proposal, thesis, or dissertation can apply the ideas in this book as long as the method of research permits explanation and inference. I have favored thinking and analysis that make explanation of phenomena possible. Descriptive, experimental, and survey research; applied and basic research; ethnographic and operant research; statistical and nonstatistical research—each has its strategic limitations, but individual authors must present their studies in convincing ways, regardless of research method. This book is about writing a convincing document. The examples on reporting the results of data analysis in Chapter 5 represent different kinds of *statistical* strategy; however, the explanatory part of Chapter 5 that precedes the examples is applicable to all methods.

2

How to Write a Thesis or Dissertation Proposal

Proposals have two major parts: (a) a problem to be investigated and (b) a method of investigation. The next few pages get you thinking about appropriate research logic and planning for a convincing proposal.

FINDING A RESEARCH TOPIC

General Subject Matter for Your Thesis

Your thesis proposal should deal with subject matter you know well. The more you know about a topic, the more likely that you will create a satisfactory proposal. The best proposals grow out of your ongoing work. These proposals are also much easier to invent because they are based on experience, and the quality of ideas and the ease of composition are natural consequences of that work history. Graduate students have the best opportunity to invent research problems when they are assistants in continuing research programs, sharing tasks and strategies with a professor who guides the research. Working on topics related to a professor's work provides a great advantage for the student who will have to generate and defend a rationale. Obviously, problems that come out of a history in ongoing work are more likely to have a defensible basis than are spontaneously generated ones.

First Steps in Finding a Research Topic

You will need to do three things in preparation for writing a proposal: (a) read published research on a topic that interests you; (b) make on-the-spot observations of the phenomena that interest you; and (c) think long and hard about how these phenomena appear to operate.

Read selectively.   One of the first things to do is search the abstracts that are published in your field. When you make that search, use key words in your current interest. For example, suppose you are interested in an aspect of artificial intelligence. You will find *artificial intelligence* listed as a key phrase in *Psychological Abstracts*. Under that term you should find recently written abstracts of articles published for a given period. Or, if you are interested in a medical topic, look for your key words in *Index Medicus*.

To prepare for research, read what are called *review articles, review journals,* and *review books*. Review articles are helpful to you as a research scholar because they organize a great deal of literature efficiently. A topical review represents the analytical thinking of some scholar who has examined existing literature, interpreted it, argued about it, and called attention to the theoretical issues it raises. These reviewers tend to be among the best scholars in their fields; that is why they are called on to write reviews.

Review journals are easy to find. Examples include the *Review of Educational Research,* published by the American Educational Research Association, and *Psychological Review,* published by the American Psychological Association. Every field of study has a source for reviews of research and theory.

In some fields of study there are books published annually that are devoted to the review of significant recent theoretical and research developments. Three such annual publications are the *Annual Review of Anthropology,* the *Annual Review of Psychology,* and the *Annual Review of Sociology.* Monographs such as *Child Development Monographs,* published by the Society for Research in Child Development, are a good source for initial reading in certain topics to get an overview.

Do not plan to generate a research problem for your thesis solely through reading. You should read, make physical observations, and think interactively from reading to observing as a basis for deriving a research problem. Don't make the mistake of writing a literature review as you read. Until a problem is fairly well identified, you should make only notes. Your literature review should then center on that identified problem. Students often write wide-ranging, irrelevant literature reviews. What you cite in your proposal should be clearly relevant to the problem you eventually identify. Introducing remotely or tangentially related literature can get in the way of clear purpose.

Make physical observations.   Take yourself bodily to a place where you can create a problem as you observe the phenomena that interest you. It is a good idea to do your thinking about a research problem while probing sources of data. With an evolving problem in mind, take paper and pencil to a place where you can observe relevant phenomena. As you read and think, probe the sources of your data in order to examine the possible dimensions or variables of a problem.

Suppose, for example, that you are interested in children's learning of time concepts. In particular, you want to know whether a child of a certain age has developed a sense of duration, or the passage of time. You might then do what Jean Piaget did—namely, invent a piece of apparatus—in his case a complex water jar with a petcock at the bottom, from which water was drained at varying rates. Piaget presented this jar and other water jars to his own children and asked them how long it might take for water to drain from one jar or another.

By varying the questions and changing his apparatus, Piaget was able to derive a problem he wanted to answer. At the same time, while Piaget was observing children's responses to his water jar apparatus, he read Immanuel Kant's treatise on time, responding to Kant's dimensions of duration, succession, simultaneity, and the like; he also read Henri Bergson's essays on time. No doubt Piaget attempted to consider everything he was reading in relation to what was occurring with his water jar apparatus. You can think of the totality of Piaget's activity as sorting out in his mind whatever he considered to be problematic for his understanding of children's development of time concepts.

This interplay of reading, observing, and thinking is a necessary part of generating useful research questions. There are certain realizations we get only from direct experience, which tell us whether we have reasonable ideas or correct concepts. Piaget did much of his work in this way. In studying cognitive development, he sat down with one of his children and proceeded to put questions to the child, while noting both the questions and the responses. One advantage to an investigator is that he or she is guided in a next question by an answer to a previous question. The investigator can think with the data and, from it, evolve suppositions about what patterns the phenomena can take. Much of Piaget's data gathering took this active form, leading the famous scientist to believe that he could find truth and establish principles in this way, and that he needed formal demonstrations ("experiments") only to convince the science community or to publicize what he had already established in private to his own satisfaction.

Avoid using the phrase *pilot study* to describe the foregoing processes. Its connotations, of a relatively formal, preplanned study, do not apply to our purpose. Remember that you are inventing a problem, not judging the feasibility of a method. To invent research, you need freedom to think and to select interesting and workable concepts. You conduct data probes or exploratory observations to find out what can be problematic for a proposal, not to test the feasibility of a problem that is already invented, as would be true of a pilot study.

What observations should you make? Here you should follow your own inventive disposition. Whether your study will be survey, description, or experimentation, you should go where you can make observations of a kind that fit with what you are reading and thinking. Because reading is always an accompaniment of observations made in the field or laboratory, it will help to guide you. Initially, many issues will seem relevant because you have not yet narrowed your search to its eventual dimensions. When you do so, you will have one issue that can be researched.

To invent research problems, graduate students need to learn how to make observations for finding problematic relations among phenomena they observe. Here are some questions you should ask when making observations to generate a proposal:

1. What combination of variables will reveal a process taking place? At what scale values of these variables?
2. When some interesting event occurs, what relation does the event have to other events?
3. How does the context effect expression of the phenomenon? When does this phenomenon occur? When does it not occur?
4. What concepts or principles help explain the phenomenon?

While reading and observing, take time to reflect.   Albert Einstein once said that young physicists would benefit by being confined to lighthouse duty. These conditions, he said, would compel a young scientist to think. Similarly, when you are contemplating a thesis or dissertation, you need quiet time to reflect on what can be made problematic among your interests. You must, of course, have something to think about. Look for patterns and associations among variables. Your thinking will often turn to questions like, "Why or when does this phenomenon occur?" Alternate reading and observation, accompanied by a lot of thinking, are the first steps in preparing to write a proposal.

WHAT IS A PROBLEM?

Before you can create a problem of your own, you must know what a research problem is. Believe it or not, that is surprisingly difficult for many students because there are no commonly accepted criteria of a satisfactory problem, and students are not generally taught how to make the judgments necessary to form satisfactory research problems.

Choosing your subject matter does not create a research problem. Subject matter, in fact, is not a criterion for deciding that you do or do not have a research problem. You cannot say, solely because you like a certain subject, that it is a research problem. Personal values are irrelevant. However, you do not have to give up your subject matter preferences. Study whatever you like, but remember that your preference for a subject does not make that subject matter problematic.

You may believe that research topics should be practical, or, on the other hand, that research should be basic, aimed at the formation of scientific laws. But when you write a proposal for research on a topic, neither of these values should enter into the language you use to express a research problem. Some people prefer biological science to physical science; others prefer behavior science to social science. But when you, as a graduate student, construct a written problem statement, none of these values will be relevant to whether your statement is satisfactory as a research problem. To understand the irrelevance of these values to research strategy, you must understand that the label *research problem* applies to a special kind of problem, different from all other problems. Research problems are explanatory devices; they are carefully crafted sentences *about finding out* and should not be intermingled with your personal or social values or with your preference for particular subject matter.

Some Criteria for a Research Problem

Calling a collection of words a research problem does not make it so. Your words must show an understanding of certain phenomena, and your proposal must have some promise of revealing convincing evidence that this understanding is correct.

This section presents a number of criteria for a satisfactory research problem. These criteria must be satisfied by the particular words you choose to express your problem. The words making up your problem statement explicitly reveal your purpose:

1. To understand a restricted set of phenomena (more restricted or limited than is commonly believed)
2. To describe the interrelations between variables that are *named in the statement*
3. To *offer in the problem statement* a potential or hypothetical solution to the problem
4. To limit the range of the problem to a single question or issue (set boundaries on the problem)

A problem statement is composed of identifiable words and sentences. A reader should be able to tell, without any difficulty, which word begins a problem statement and which word ends it. As a proposal writer, you should choose your words carefully to gain as precise a meaning as possible. Ordinarily, a single paragraph of a few sentences is sufficient to express the central concepts of a problem. This is followed by auxiliary statements that elaborate and explain the problem.

For reasons that are explained more fully at the beginning of Chapter 7, you should go directly to a problem in the first sentence of page 1. Resist the temptation to give background or set the stage for your problem. Your professors and other readers will prefer to know immediately what your study will be about. They will not want to search for a problem statement. Nothing you can say will better prepare your readers for the content of your proposal than a problem statement given at the very beginning.

To be effective, your opening words should be arresting and clear:

> (a) In this study I intend to find evidence that . . . (b) This will be an investigation of the [such and such] effect observed by [so and so]. In those observations she or he found [a certain phenomenon] that has not yet been explained. The problem in this study is to show that the [phenomenon] can be explained by a relation between variables [X and Y].

Continue until the problem is fully explicated for readers. Of course, the words and phrases you can use to begin your proposal are limitless, but you should choose those that get right at the purpose of the study.

A problem statement is composed entirely of words about finding out and contains no words justifying a topic of investigation. Researchers investigate research problems to come to an understanding of something, to create and organize knowledge. This is the central purpose of research, and it is not easily combined with other purposes. The words you write to represent a research problem should be words that have *investigative* meaning—sentences about discovering or finding out, not sentences about possible application of the results or the potential importance of the findings.

So many students miss this point that it seems wise to pause here to reemphasize it: Problem statements are *composed entirely of words about finding out* and contain no words justifying the topic of investigation.

Here are some effective and appropriate ways to begin a problem statement. They can be the very first words of a proposal.

In this study I intend to [one of the following]:

1. Get evidence that [such and such] is true.
2. Find out whether [explanation A] is superior to [explanation B].
3. Test a supposition that the policies of school management seldom include curricular rules or philosophy.
4. Put [so and so's] theory to test at the juncture of variables [A and B, at certain scale values]. I will argue that the theory is untenable at that juncture.

Personal and social problems are not, in themselves, research problems. Increases in crime or drug use, children's failure to learn, poverty—these are all important problems. But the relevance of any of them to research is remote and unknown. The vital importance of a practical issue, its relevance to society, have nothing to do with whether it meets the definition of a research problem. To understand the concept of a research problem, then, you would do well to disassociate the personal and social problems that concern you from your definition of a research problem.

Here is an illustration of a failed attempt to create a research problem. Let the following paragraph represent a student's effort to express a problem to be researched:

> An alarming number of adults in the United States are unable to read. Jones (1991) has reported a survey covering the entire nation which shows that 22 percent of the population over age 20 cannot read fifth-grade text. Although many people believe that reading failures are due to insufficient emphasis on reading in the schools, there is no generally accepted explanation for the large number of adult nonreaders. In the study I am proposing, I will examine approximately 13 new clients who enter each week to begin reading instruction at the Urban Reading Clinic. In my study I will give these new clients The Comprehension Inventory, a diagnostic device meant to identify bases for failure to read. The inventory lists 8 general classes of reading performance and 36 specific aspects of comprehension that can be estimated in a person taking the inventory. If I am able to group the subjects of my study according to the general and specific classes of comprehension failure, it may then be possible to infer the basis on which these persons failed to learn to read in the first place.

Notice how general this statement is; it merely calls attention to a social problem that exists in the United States. Although the writer apparently believes that the *unexplained* aspect of the social problem helps to define it as a research problem, in fact, nothing about the foregoing statement gives it researchable qualities. It lacks even the most basic requirement of a research problem.

Many graduate students will be surprised by such a complete condemnation. They may respond favorably to the simplicity of the statement—and they are right, in that the statement is easy to follow. They may believe that the proposed study is likely to have practical value because it refers to an important real-world problem. But their interpretation is wrong. Reading behavior is such an enormously complex subject that there is virtually no chance that by looking through the inventory records of 100 or even 1,000 people, one would find something conceptual that could be used to solve a real-life problem in reading.

Herein lies a basic principle of writing about research problems: *Never make value judgments or statements asserting the usefulness of your planned research.* The statement of what you consider to be a researchable problem must carry its own justification. Phrases like "critical issue" or "crucial problem" are unwarranted claims that almost certainly exaggerate. It may, however, be appropriate to refer to a theory or hypothesis as "important" if the word *important* points to a key juncture between variables or to a truly important link between theories. *Importance means heuristic importance*—importance that has to do with discovering.

A research problem is narrower than most social problems.   The breadth of social problems makes it nearly impossible to foresee their solutions. Research problems are much narrower. Expressions of research problems contain suppositions about their solutions, and this is possible only because research problems are limited. True, sometimes people do propose solutions to broad social problems, but those solutions are not research solutions; that is, the operations involved in solving the problems are not those an investigator would perform in studying a research problem. The purpose of research is to *understand* and *explain.*

In engineering and other technical fields, an entire solution is seldom foreseen all at once. In cases where only the general form of a solution can be anticipated, an investigator will attack one subproblem at a time. These subproblems in research and development are similar to research problems in other fields of study. The practical issue is first broken down into problems of manageable size, and the resulting problems involve finding out or explaining phenomena. To have the necessary research characteristics, a problem statement should explain a relation between variables.

A problem statement is a statement about relations among variables. All problem statements refer to variables, and problem statements refer to relations that link these variables together in some orderly way. Relations between variables are *problematic*—that is, they represent research problems—because the proposal writer argues for the existence of such relations and proposes to get further evidence. This simply means that the researcher believes that two or more variables of interest are related, either simply or in a complex way, and offers that supposition as a basis for doing an investigation. An investigator therefore must invent a means of obtaining data that either strengthen or weaken confidence in that supposition. Keep in mind that this discussion deals with what the actual words of a problem statement say. *The words must speak about variables and the relations that join them.*

Each of the following sentence fragments refers to a variable:

1. Determine *how many errors* occur when . . .
2. To find that the *rate of response* is likely to be . . .
3. The *density of adjectives* is diminished by . . .
4. Measure the *brightness of the light* after . . .
5. Then the *age at which a child is first able to* . . .
6. And finding the *number of genes* to be . . .
7. However, the *amount of attention paid to* . . .

And here are sentence fragments containing more than one variable with a relation joining them:

8. The *velocity* is inversely related to *temperature* of . . .
9. So that *gender* bears no relation to *speed with which* . . .
10. Then the *time required to respond* is proportional to the *loudness* of . . .

A problem statement has more to do with what is known than with what is not known. To learn what the term *research problem* means, you must know what it does not mean. The word *problem* does not mean that there are multiple unexplained and unidentified relations somewhere among certain variables, nor is a research proposal an offer to seek out some unknown relation, nor is it the suggestion that such a relation may somehow emerge from your investigation. A research problem is already problematic at the time the proposal is written. That is, you already know enough to say what the hypothetical relations are.

In inferential statistics, we refer to one- and two-tailed questions. In one-tailed questions there is some basis for explaining the form of a relation (for example, to start with the claim that *A* is greater than *B,* and then subsequently get statistical evidence that *A > B).* One-tailed questions are expressions of what we know in substance; two-tailed questions are, in effect, expressions of ignorance (for example, either *A > B* or *B > A,* but there is insufficient basis for predicting an outcome). Two-tailed questions are not problematic in the research sense; they are not a good basis for a research proposal. Research problems should contain in their written expression some potential solution.

The foregoing is not meant to exclude all two-tailed questions from research. To some degree they are acceptable in an investigator's preliminary thinking. But professors and students cannot blindly agree to conduct research; to formulate an acceptable problem, an investigator must do preliminary work to get beyond simple empirical questions (or two-tailed questions). Professors prefer a proposal that presents a well-developed problem if they are to agree to the investigation.

A problem statement has elements of its own solution.   Generation of a problem may be the most significant and creative aspect of doing research. You create a research problem through a tentative belief, often called a *supposition* or a *hypothesis.* A research problem has no prior existence; it is not "there" waiting to be discovered. Rather, it must be created as an expression of possible relations among variables. Positive belief, though tentative, is the creative expression of one or more supposed relations. These hypothetical relations place limits or boundaries on a research problem. This means that phenomena are problematic in the research sense only when you already know enough to foresee how these phenomena might be organized. The supposed relations are nonetheless problematic because a degree of uncertainty exists concerning the empirical verification of the hypothesized relations among variables.

As a student investigator, you should develop a problem to the point of hypothesizing relations among variables before you attempt to write a proposal. Your proposal should anticipate a certain hypothetical structure among variables. The problem may be based on a single hypothesis or on two or three interdependent ones.

Graduate students should not be intimidated by this need to form hypotheses and to create order from apparent confusion. It takes time and continual reworking of ideas to develop research problems from simple questions. Usually you will have to revise and clarify what you write.

Your beliefs about the supposed relations among variables should be progressive. As you probe data sources, read, and think about the problem, possible relations among variables are likely to come up. Some of them will remain convincing under scrutiny; others will not. In either case, you should examine them until some promising order appears. As your knowledge and understanding increase, your belief will grow as well.

Research proposals should hold the promise of integrating already existing knowledge. Proposals organize what is known to show what remains to be organized as new knowledge. Some hypothetical relation may, through your research, become more believable.

A problem statement has a singular focus—a single set of hypothetical relations.   Research problems are narrow. They have boundaries. When a problem is stated, the statement should make the limits of that problem obvious. One way to do this is to see what kind of data will satisfy the problem as evidence. If the data will be of so many different kinds that they do not converge to a common set of arguments, that may mean that the problem is not one, but many problems. A research problem should relate to data in syllogistic fashion: If *A,* then *B;* if a specific problem, then data specifically related to that problem. A vague problem can accept data of many kinds, and there will be no objective relation joining the problem to the particular data.

This discussion is centered on the invention of a *limited* problem (remember, if it isn't limited, it isn't a problem). We continue to pursue the question of what makes a research problem and what, in particular, gives a problem singularity. No research problem exists until the problem seeker can express a problem as a singular issue.

The following is an example of a nonproblem, because its statement lacks boundaries:

> I will examine a relation between social development in children and these children's ability patterns.

Here is an incomplete example of a bounded expression that can be part of a problem statement:

> I offer a hypothesis that stress-inducing changes in family structure result in greater impairment of social than of intellectual functioning. The greater impairment of social functions occurs because . . .

How will you know if you have a singular or unified problem? When one, two, or three—but seldom more than three—closely related hypotheses can represent the problem, it has unity. It is preferable to have interrelated hypotheses, such that the truth of one makes more likely the truth of the others.

If, after making a reasonable effort, you cannot offer any promising hypotheses, that may mean that the topic and its questions are not ready for investigation. If you are to create appropriate research operations, there must already exist a context of suitable theory and usable research techniques. If insufficient knowledge exists on a topic, you should seek a more limited question that is manageable by research. Do not be reluctant to reduce a seemingly important but unwieldy question to one that can be studied.

When Your Proposal Lacks a Singular Focus

This section deals with proposals that lack specificity, problem statements that do not have singularity. If the words of your intended problem statement are too general, in effect you are saying to your mentor, "Trust me, I'll find something to investigate as I look around and get some data."

Avoid the look-around-the-barn concept of a problem. Identifying a research problem is more than taking a stroll through the barn to see what turns up. In proposing research, it is not enough to say that you will look in certain places and consider certain variables. This is too vague and general to serve as a *research problem.* Looking around is not evidence of a problem, although it does have the potential to disclose many unidentified problems.

Some people think that anything puzzling or enigmatic amounts to a research problem. But a research problem is not just any set of unidentified relations. If research problems could be conceptualized in this way, a "problem" would be not a single problem, but any number of possible enigmas.

In an earlier example, a problem statement dealt with the unexplained inability of many adults to read. The statement, "There is no generally accepted explanation for the large number of adult nonreaders," implies that this lack of explanation somehow makes the issue a candidate for research. The writer also said: "If I am able to group the subjects of my study according to the general and specific classes of comprehension failure, it may then be possible to infer the basis on which these persons failed to learn to read in the first place." What this writer was really saying is: "I intend to take a look around, with the use of *The*

A singular problem is a statement read by several readers who agree they have identified in the statement:

1. A particular association of variables that all readers recognize (when asked for the focus of a study, all name the same variables)
2. A hypothetical relation or set of relations among variables having a supposed form or direction (a form all readers identify and agree on); this means that the statement tells how the variables intersect or come together
3. Boundaries of a problem that make obvious what the problem's limits are
4. A basis for a solution and the ability to see in the problem what kind of evidence a solution requires

A research problem is not a statement:

1. Referring to general problems
2. Claiming practical consequences
3. Justifying or expressing the importance of a problem (never containing words like *critical, crucial,* or *vital,* which exaggerate in all but true life-and-death circumstances)
4. Focusing mainly on the unknown or mysterious

Comprehension Inventory, and, should I find the observations classifiable, the classifications may provide a basis for inferring a cause of reading failure."

Remember that research problems are statements expressing knowledge about what a solution may be and what may explain relevant phenomena. This proposal writer should have identified a hypothetical cause for reading failure as a basis for writing a proposal, and made that hypothesis the central point of a plan of study.

Although thesis proposals generally need a hypothesis, a plausible one about reading failure in this case is very unlikely. Think in these terms: Millions of children are learning to read, and thousands of people are teaching them. If a hypothesis could readily be invented to explain failure in reading comprehension, one of those teachers would have formed that hypothesis and presented the evidence for it long ago. Most common personal and social problems that have ready solutions are solved in the normal course of events. When they are not solved, we can assume that the problem is too difficult and usually too broad for a simple solution.

GENERATING A RESEARCH PROBLEM AND VERIFYING ITS CONTENT

Figures 2.1 and 2.2 are intended to help you identify the necessary content of a problem statement. Figure 2.1 refers to an investigator's generative activities before forming a problem, called "preproblem developments" in Figure 2.1. Figure 2.2 is used to verify that you have written a problem statement. Many proposals, and even some research reports, do not contain the problem statements writers believe they have written.

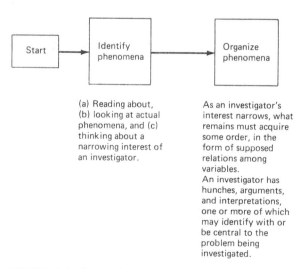

FIGURE 2.1 Generating a research problem prior to formalizing that problem in a proposal.

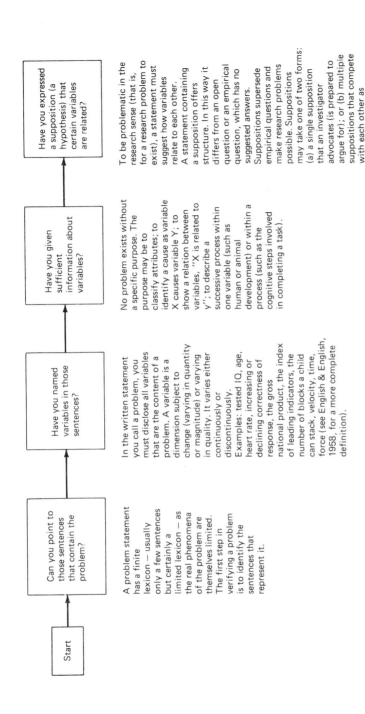

| Start | Can you point to those sentences that contain the problem? | Have you named variables in those sentences? | Have you given sufficient information about variables? | Have you expressed a supposition (a hypothesis) that certain variables are related? |

A problem statement has a finite lexicon — usually only a few sentences but certainly a limited lexicon — as the real phenomena of the problem are themselves limited. The first step in verifying a problem is to identify the sentences that represent it.

In the written statement you call a problem, you must disclose all variables that are the content of a problem. A variable is a dimension subject to change (varying in quantity or magnitude) or varying in quality. It varies either continuously or discontinuously. Examples: tested IQ, age, heart rate, increasing or declining correctness of response, the gross national product, the index of leading indicators, the number of blocks a child can stack, velocity, time, force (see English & English, 1958, for a more complete definition).

No problem exists without a specific purpose. The purpose may be to classify attributes; to identify a cause as variable X causes variable Y; to show a relation between variables, "X is related to y"; to describe a successive process within one variable (such as human or animal development) or within a process (such as the cognitive steps involved in completing a task).

To be problematic in the research sense (that is, for a research problem to exist), a statement must suggest how variables relate to each other. A statement containing a supposition offers a supposition offers structure. In this way it differs from an open question or an empirical question, which has no suggested answers. Suppositions supersede empirical questions and make research problems possible. Suppositions may take one of two forms: (a) a single supposition that an investigator advocates (is prepared to argue for); or (b) multiple suppositions that compete with each other as potential explanations of the same phenomena. In the second case, an investigator may or may not be an advocate for one of the suppositions.

FIGURE 2.2 Verifying that you have written a problem.

19

CONDUCTING A LIBRARY SEARCH

As you begin your research, make good records of your work and your thinking. Two kinds of records that will save time by prompting you as you write are *litera-ture citations,* written when you find them, together with notes made on them, and *concepts about research problems,* written as notes (naming the variables, ideas about relations, and so on).

Form of Literature Citations

Make it a rule to record complete citations for every piece of literature you re-view. Use either full or half sheets of $8\frac{1}{2}''$ × $11''$ paper (or $5''$ × $8''$ cards) to record single citations—*only one* citation per sheet. Put the bibliographic information at the top in exactly the form you will use in the reference list at the end of your proposal and your thesis. Don't abbreviate, and always write your citations in the correct form for the final product.

Because you can alphabetize these reference sheets by shuffling them, it is easy to insert or delete references at any time. Both for your proposal and for the actual thesis, pull out those reference sheets that you have decided to make part of your written composition. They will automatically constitute a reference list for you to type in the form already written, so you will not have to duplicate your work. Avoid thinking that you'll complete the bibliographic information later. Avoid the common criticism that students are apt to cite references that are not in their reference list.

To create a correct reference list, you will need the form manual accepted for your field of study. The *Publication Manual of the American Psychological Association,* third edition (1983), is one such manual. Suppose, for example, that you wish to cite the authors of one chapter in an edited book that includes chap-ters by many other authors. According to the APA *Publication Manual,* 3rd ed. (p. 125), the following is a correct citation:

Hartley, J. T., Harker, J. O., & Walsh, D. A. (1980). Contemporary issues and new directions in adult development of learning and memory. In L. W. Poon (Ed.), *Aging in the 1980s: Psychologi-cal issues* (pp. 239–252). Washington, DC: American Psychological Association.

The space remaining after a citation on each $5''$ × $8''$ card is for your notes—your abstract of the work. If one card is insufficient for your notes on a book or a complex article, use more cards attached to each other. You need to use skill and judgment in deciding what to write. Try to record the central ideas and those related to your current thinking. As long as you write the complete citation, you can go back to the reference if you fail to note something essential. Writing these notes will provoke ideas that in turn will contribute to the forma-tion of your research problem.

Notes about Concepts, Variables, and Problems

In addition to the notes you append to literature citations, keep a notebook for notes reflecting your own observations and thinking. Like your literature notes, these observations of real phenomena will help you formulate your research problem. When you think your ideas can be written in the form of a problem, attempt a problem statement in this notebook. You may find it useful to refer back to these successive efforts when you write your actual proposal and your final research report. Even if your early efforts do not stand up to your continuing examination and critical judgment, they may eventually lead to a problem and are often helpful in writing a rationale for a proposal and for the thesis itself. Don't trust your memory. Make writing easier for yourself by recording ideas you can modify for later use.

DECIDING ON STATISTICAL ANALYSES

Don't leave decisions about the form of analysis until last. There are published decision trees to help you choose appropriate statistical analyses to fit your data (e.g., Andrews, Klem, Davidson, O'Malley, & Rodgers, 1975; Stock & Dodenhoff, 1982; Uhl, 1972). Stock and Dodenhoff have three large decision trees to help investigators choose a form of statistical analysis.

Whether or not your strategy is statistical, you should think about what you intend to demonstrate and what form your arguments can take (how the data will be grouped or organized for analysis). Your ideas about strategy will help guide your investigation.

WRITING YOUR FIRST DRAFT

You must always follow the directions and preferences of your mentor and any standards set by an academic department. They have responsibility for the quality of your work; they will give you direction, but you must ask what is expected. Research writing has special requirements, treated in Chapter 7. Read that chapter before writing so as to avoid the errors graduate students often make. For example, the popular use of the present tense of verbs is often unsuitable for research writing. In your proposal, you should use the past tense to refer to past research: "Johnson *found* that," not "Johnson *finds* that."

Length

A concise proposal should be your goal. Avoid aimless, rambling discourse that fails to identify a problem. Such aimlessness is an annoyance to any graduate committee. To avoid this difficulty, follow the advice on organization in Chapter 7 and the heuristic structure given in Chapter 3 on introductions.

Write a short first draft. Unless directed otherwise, limit your first draft to somewhere between three and seven pages. Ask your major professor if you may have his or her reaction to a very short preproposal. If so, give these pages your very best thinking. Start with two or three sentences that express the heart of your problem, and be as direct as possible.

There are two reasons for this short draft. You will be better able to tell how clear your thinking is if you first write a short statement. Few students can write more on their first try and have the paper turn out well. Moreover, your major professor can more easily identify your intentions and direct you from such a short draft. Your second draft may be somewhat longer, but you should still guard against rambling and irrelevancies.

Writing a short paper requires that you focus on the most essential ideas and examine closely how well you can express them. When you have talked over this first paper with the professor, you will have a list of suggestions of what to do next. You will almost certainly discover strategic flaws you didn't foresee. How, then, would you respond if you had written twenty pages?

To save time for yourself and your committee, first get the essence of a problem and work out an approximate method. When you see how others analyze just that much, you will know what to change and be better able to take the next steps. Along with this first short draft, present separately to your committee the empirical observations you made while generating the problem.

Hard as it may be to accept, a first draft can almost never be preserved intact. Making several revisions is the norm. Even a proposal accepted by your committee, although it will be a great help, should not be carried forward intact as the first part of your thesis. By the time you write the thesis, the problem may have changed, and you certainly will have a more interesting repertoire from which to write.

Literature Review

Should you add or omit a separate section called "Literature Review"? Ask your professors if they will allow you to put *all* literature citations with *problem-relevant ideas* in the proposal's introduction. This will mean that you have no separate section called "Literature Review"; your proposal will have two main parts: an introduction (problem statement) and a section on method. Fitting the literature citations into your introduction will help you select only those citations that best fit your rationale.

PRODUCING A PROPOSAL, FROM BEGINNING TO WRITTEN PRODUCT

Seeing the Whole Process

Figure 2.3 shows the whole process of preparing a proposal, from first conceptions to finished document. It is a flow diagram with three main processes: (a) inventing a research problem before writing a proposal, (b) writing explanatory and operational expressions of a problem containing one or more suppositions and all the presuppositions that argue for each supposition and (c) writing a method. These processes are listed across the top of Figure 2.3.

To interpret Figure 2.3, follow the solid arrows horizontally from "Start" at the far left to the box "Identify order." These are the successive steps in developing a research problem. The vertical lines connect them to interactive processes that work both ways. An investigator analyzes data probes and library searches interactively until he or she is able to select the phenomena to be studied. As a student investigator, you should interpret empirical and literature relations by comparing them and ultimately finding in these relations a supposed order that

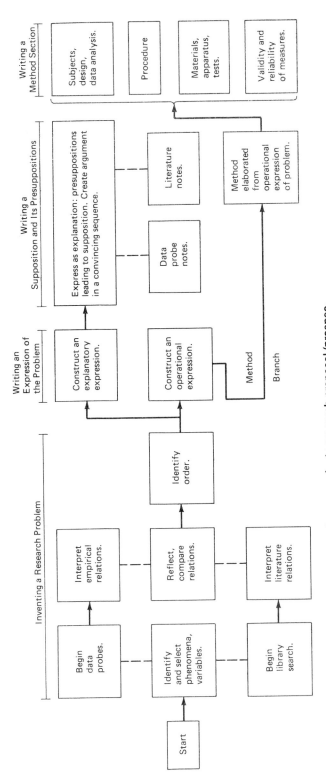

FIGURE 2.3 Flow chart of steps taken to produce a graduate research proposal (prospectus). Follow arrows from "Inventing a Research Problem" to "Writing an Expression of the Problem.

23

will be the basis for writing your proposal. Notice that the heading "Inventing a Research Problem" at the top of the figure ends with "Identify order." This means that a supposed order has emerged among the variables and the investigator is ready to write an expression of that problem.

The written expression of a problem has two parts, an explanatory expression and an operational expression (treated in Chapter 3). They are both heuristic concepts (aspects of discovery) as well as expository concepts (mechanisms of explanation).

The explanatory and operational expressions of problems are complementary expressions; you need both in your proposal. Chapter 3 on writing research introductions defines these two kinds of problem expression and tells how to compose them. Use Chapter 3 as a guide in writing the introduction to your proposal.

AN EXAMPLE INTRODUCTION TO A PROPOSAL

Proposal introductions are similar to thesis introductions.   The introductions to proposals and theses share the same content and form; both expose and explain a research problem. The only difference is that when you write the final report, you may have greater understanding and may write with greater insight. But the form of the exposition and its general content can be the same in both.

The brief example of an introduction to a proposal that follows was created from an article by Russac (1978) that appeared in the journal *Child Development*. The example proposal is entirely fictional; that is, the content was created here to illustrate concepts important to a proposal. Russac's article was used because it has qualities that make it appropriate as an illustration. Although Russac is responsible for the published article, he bears no responsibility for this proposal.

Running parallel with the example proposal is a commentary.   The proposal is in the left column, with a commentary in the right column. The commentary may be especially beneficial, as it contains interpretations graduate committee members often make.

A Proposal to Study the Development of
Two Representations of Cardinal Number in Young Children
Proposal Writer X
The University of Good Intentions

In this proposed study I intend to show that children demonstrate an understanding of cardinal numbers by counting before they demonstrate such knowledge by putting objects in one-to-one correspondence (placing objects in pairs without counting so that two collections have equal numbers). If, in this study, I can show which of these two number abilities appears

Have an effective title. If possible, disclose in your title the variables you will study. Unlike reports of finished work, proposals usually allow longer titles when necessary to convey the essential ideas. Perhaps the title for this study might read: "A Proposal to Study in Children the Development of a Cardinal Number Con-

first, that will reveal how extensively small children understand cardinality.

The cardinal number concept is complex and likely to be gained one ramification at a time, until the concept is well developed. Although a cardinal number *is* a certain quantity and means that quantity, any such quantity is associated with other equal quantities (they have the same cardinal number) and can be compared to lesser and greater quantities. Moreover, cardinality is intimately tied up with concepts of conservation of quantity. Any child who knows the cardinal concept can demonstrate with either task, counting or correspondence, an understanding of equal, inferior, and superior collections of objects. If his knowledge is complete, he can conserve that quantity also.

Although small children are likely to be better at counting than at putting objects in correspondence, if I am wrong-if my subjects determine cardinal numbers equally well by counting and by correspondence-that will be evidence that they progress from premediational to mediational thought more quickly than I and some others believe (Jones, 1987; Wilson, 1989) [fictional]). Should the abilities appear equal, then this early demonstration of one-to-one correspondence, a task these children probably have not tried before, will show that they have a generalized and elaborated concept of cardinality; they will then recognize *equal* and *not equal* in a new task.

Although I see no reason to expect such mediation, Gelman and Gallistel (1986) have had much to say about what they believe is an underestimation of children's knowledge of number. This is not to say that Gelman and Gallistel have claimed that small children mediate equalities in a correspondence task. They have, however, emphasized that others underestimate children's quantitative understanding. Then, should my subjects do as well in a correspondence task as in counting, I will take that as evidence favoring Gelman and Gallistel and, additionally, as evidence that these children are able to mediate concepts of *equal* and *not equal*.

Cardinality concepts probably appear first in counting because children learn to count before they learn other number operations. I have assumed that counting is initially rote and imitative in small children. Parents practice counting with their children to teach them how to arrive at a quantity, but these parents do

cept by Counting and by One-to-One Correspondence.''

Provide a by-line. Use your name as author, omitting the word *by*. It is acceptable to list your college or university in a by-line.

State the problem first. This first paragraph focuses a reader's attention on the heart of the proposed study by beginning immediately with the problem to be studied. The very first sentence does much to convey to a reader just what the proposed study will be about. Always begin proposals in this way so that your mentors will not have to search for the central ideas. Notice that variables are given: (a) order by age, and (b) two representations of cardinal number, by counting and by one-to-one correspondence. The first paragraph contains the principal supposition (hypothesis) that counting is likely to develop first. Often a hypothesis can be expressed early to good effect, whether written formally or informally.

Now for the important question: Is there a problem here? Yes, it can be expressed as a question: Which comes first in concept formation, cardinal number by counting or cardinal number by one-to-one correspondence? Supposedly the answer is "by counting." The explanatory content of the problem continues, but the most important elements are in the very first paragraph of the proposal. To be certain you can see what motivated the writer, read Chapter 7 on organizing.

Give an explanatory problem statement. The explanation opposite is a discussion of the relevance of the research question to theory. The writer has anticipated results that will agree or disagree with his supposition (hypothesis). Over the succeeding pages, the author has pointed out that children need time to form concepts and that these concepts have a basis in a child's experience. Small children generally practice counting, but not one-to-one correspondence, which embodies the concepts of *equal, more,* and *less.*

Graduate research proposals need explanation. They need explanation of the place of a prob-

not provide similar rote practice at placing objects in pairs (one-to-one correspondence) to obtain a cardinal number.

Even if a child correctly places objects in pairs to show equal numbers in two collections, the correct answer is limited in what it demonstrates about a child's understanding of quantity. The correspondence test can be made to show that a child can compare collections of objects for equal, not equal, more, and fewer; but the test is less direct in revealing what a child knows about absolute quantities (a cardinal number). For example, the one-to-one correspondence test is not evidence that a child knows the meaning of *nine* or of *nineness;* rather, it shows that a child knows that a collection of nine is equal to another collection of nine. Emphasis on a concept of *equal* may sacrifice the cardinal concept (the absolute value of number).

Counting, on the other hand, is directed toward obtaining an absolute quantity; at least, that is true of most of the practice in early childhood. Counting is aimed toward calling out the cardinal number at the end of a counted series (e.g., ''Here there's three.''). Thus, there is reason to think that small children will learn the absolute value of a number before they learn its comparative value. Children do, of course, compare quantities by counting, but these comparisons are delayed until a child can express cardinal values.

Cardinal number, as opposed to ordinal number, represents quantity. For example, there are 14 words in the title of this proposal; 14 is a cardinal number, a quantity representing the collection of words in the title. Bertrand Rus-

lem in theory or the relevance a study will have to existing knowledge. These paragraphs set out inferences about what children are likely to understand about cardinal numbers (quantities) and show the writer's thoroughness in thinking the problem through.

Notice the amount of explanation here. A proposal should explain enough to show that the author has come to understand the phenomena in question. Analysis and interpretation demonstrate mastery of the concepts and provide a basis for explanatory suppositions.

The type of problem determines what can be explained. In this proposal, there is a lot of well-developed theory that the author was able to weave into the discussion or explanation. Had the study been, say, a survey of attitudes, a well-developed theory surrounding the attitudes in question might not exist. The explanation of the problem would then be shorter, but the investigator must provide sufficient explanation to convince his or her mentor that the study is worth doing.

Is the discussion appropriate to the problem? When the discussion coheres and the concepts fit together, the introduction as a whole creates a complete picture of the writer's purpose and beliefs about the research phenomena under examination.

Is the discussion understandable? That depends to some degree on a readers' knowledge of basic number theory, but the ideas are not too complex for the average graduate student to follow. The vocabulary is not arcane; despite the use of an occasional technical term, for the most part the words are ordinary. Good expository writers will make a conscious effort to avoid affectation and arcane, ponderous expressions. Complex ideas, however, are not easy to convey simply in writing, and are not always easy to read and understand.

Define technical terms. In a tradition that is sometimes still followed, proposals and theses contain a formal section near the beginning entitled ''Definition of Terms.'' Whether or not your

sell (1937, pp. 111-116) provided a precise logical definition of cardinal number by means of what he called ''one-one relation,'' now commonly called one-to-one correspondence. Russell said that a definition by the operations of counting is very complex and only somewhat satisfactory. Nonetheless, one-to-one correspondence and counting are the two mathematical operations that are commonly recognized as means of establishing a cardinal number to stand for a quantity.

Hypothesis 1: Cardinal Number Develops in Counting before Correspondence.

My proposed study is centered on a hypothesis 1: that in the age range from 5 to 7, children are better able to determine a cardinal number through counting (enumeration) than they are through one-to-one correspondence. That greater understanding children have of counting operations applies to equalities, to inequalities, and to transitivity. This hypothesis does not imply that children who give correct cardinal representations for small collections have a complete and satisfactory concept of such a quantity.

Prehypotheses on Which the Hypothesis Is Based

Prehypothesis 1: A concept of quantity is more explicit in counting than in one-to-one correspondence. As objects are counted, the one who counts observes a successive increase in the quantity being counted that is exactly related to the numbers called. The vocalizations and hand movements are accompanied by an explicit demonstration of what is meant by quantity (that is, a numeral 2 means 2 units; next in order, 3 means the quantity 3, and so on; and although these are numbers in transit toward the cardinal number, each can be interpreted as a quantity).

If there are approximations to quantitative meanings of correspondence, those approximations are subtle. Objects taken in pairs represent equality of two quantities, but the physical operations do not explicitly demonstrate an absolute quantity. Thus, seven pairs is a subtle representation of the meaning *seven*.

Prehypothesis 2: Other things being equal,

mentors require it (and most no longer do), make sure the central terms in your discussion are generally understood and not controversial or, if not, that you define them in the discourse. The term *cardinal number* is, of course, central to the present proposal, and there is enough uncertainty about its definition to warrant special discussion.

Here is the principal hypothesis. A hypothesis or supposition is an expository device; it is the most succinct possible expression of your problem. The adjacent hypothesis could have been placed first in the proposal, introducing an explanatory problem statement. The very first paragraph does contain a preliminary and more abstract expression of the hypothesis than is found in the formal statement opposite. You can decide where exactly to place a formal hypothesis, but it should appear near the beginning of your introduction, because hypotheses are excellent recruiters of ideas, and early placement gets readers on track. An explanatory expression of a problem should include at least one supposition.

Prehypotheses are the bases of hypotheses. Committee members are likely to ask, as they should: Why do you hold this hypothesis? The answer is found in your prehypotheses or presuppositions. Whether or not you explicitly identify them as prehypotheses, they are essential. It is not reasonable to express a hypothesis without explaining its basis. In the paragraphs headed "Prehypothesis 1," "Prehypothesis 2," and "Prehypothesis 3," the first sentence of each paragraph expresses a presupposition or prehypothesis. The sentences that follow explain and elaborate (see Chapter 3, p. 56).

When students are confused about what a *pre*hypothesis is, they usually express an idea that is identical with the hypothesis or has only trivial differences in meaning. One should always ask: "Why do I believe this hypothesis?" The answers (there are usually multiple reasons) are your prehypotheses.

children will more easily learn those conceptual tasks that can be learned gradually in a simplified sequence of steps. Sometimes parents first teach children to vocalize a series of numbers before teaching them to count objects. Vocalizing the numbers is not a manifestation of quantitative knowledge, but it is a helpful prerequisite. Parents next teach children to associate the vocalizations with objects. When such associations succeed, parents infer that their children are acquiring a concept of quantity. Practice continues in school, and by the second grade most of what children know about quantities has a counting association.

Prehypothesis 3: Children are unlikely to have early experience with one-to-one correspondence. The numerical reason for taking objects in pairs is to ensure equal-sized groupings of objects. Spatial organization of objects in pairs in order to show equality or inequality is what is meant by one-to-one correspondence. Until children understand the concept of equal numbers of objects, they are unlikely to use one-to-one correspondence to mean a certain number of objects.

Prehypothesis 4: A numerical concept of equality by one-to-one correspondence is both too advanced and too abstract for most parents to consider teaching to their children. Perhaps even when parents do understand the mathematical purpose of a one-to-one concept, they still will not resort to it in teaching because they themselves have made greater use of counting. In everyday experience, the correspondence task has little use; therefore, a parent is unlikely to think of demonstrating equality by correspondence.

Hypothesis 2: Conservation of Number Is More Difficult than Other Cardinal Representations

Hypothesis 2 is a minor hypothesis because the aggregation of prior evidence in its favor is so well established as to leave little doubt. Previous investigations and the interpretations of many observers show that conservation of number will be at least as difficult as any of the correspondence tasks (Gelman & Gallistel, 1986; Piaget, 1968; Russac, 1978).

Although this logic is simple, unfortunately, it is seldom easy to construct the bases for a hypothesis in a proposal. Most people must think long and hard about them and usually must rework and revise their explanations to improve their clarity and precision.

When should you cite the work of others? Does the adjacent text need more documentation? That depends on whether the ideas need citations to make them believable and whether published sources exist that say just what the writer intends to say. Follow this principle: Assume that your readers will examine the original of every citation you list, and that, in consequence all citations should seem reasonable in their context. Citations should be directly applicable to the text where they appear. Good scholarship includes honesty of intention; every citation should be directly relevant, not just added to give a false impression of thoroughness.

How might committee members regard the low density of citations in the adjacent text? Because the ideas have their own internal logic, it is likely that readers will be able to judge their reasonableness without resort to some other authority. Later, however, under the heading "Context of the Problem," is a discussion that should contain more literature citations. The density of relevant citations should be higher there because the content requires it. The most important factor is not the number of citations, but whether each is relevant and justifiable. Your own ideas hold a special place in a proposal, and those ideas benefit from citations only if they add to your own thinking or show agreement or disagreement with you.

Number of hypotheses. Hypothesis 2, opposite, is a minor hypothesis, a logical extension of the first. Research reports that interpret and integrate concepts are usually based on a small number of related hypotheses. Don't write hypotheses for every question to which you think your data apply. It will only confuse readers about what the research problem is. One, two, or three hypotheses are almost always enough to represent a singular problem. Convincing proposals are based on integrated

Relation of the Problem to Concept Formation and to Number Theory

One might ask: What demonstrations by children give the best and least ambiguous evidence of an understanding of cardinal number? No response shows complete understanding. Perhaps the least ambiguous is *subitizing,* a name given to the process of looking at a small collection and, without counting, giving a cardinal number to represent it. To illustrate, suppose three objects are presented to a child, and the child is asked for a number. The answer, three, is a cardinal number unconfounded with serial numbers (in counting, the meaning of serial vocalizations is confounded with the meaning of a cardinal number). The difficulty with subitizing is that children can visually encompass no more than 5 or 6 objects, but practice up to those numbers probably represents cardinality well.

The cardinal concept is the concept of a *number prototype,* a hypothetical mental construct representing all collections having the same number of objects; then all collections of the same number are said to be equal. Cardinal equalities are best represented by one-to-one correspondence. One-to-one correspondence tasks have the sole purpose of showing that two collections are equal or not equal.

Piaget and Szeminska (1965) believed that conservation of number is the best criterion of a child's understanding of cardinal number. That interpretation follows a test they made after a child had established one-to-one correspondence for two sets. A child was first asked to confirm that two collections were, in fact, equal collections. If the child confirmed that they were equal, one set was spread out or reduced in space (transformed to appear larger or smaller) and the child was again asked about the sets being equal, larger, or smaller. A correct interpretation of cardinal number for the two quantities requires that a child will know that a collection of objects does not lose its quantitative integrity when it is transformed in some number-irrelevant way.

Piaget contended that a test of conservation of number is a sufficiently sensitive test of the meaning of quantity. He believed that to understand conservation, a child must understand both cardinality and ordinality. According to him, when comparing two sets for their equality, one must simultaneously consider the two aggre-

ideas, in which everything fits together well. A long list of hypotheses betrays lack of purpose or lack of a rationale for the research. How can a problem contain many suppositions within it? It isn't likely if the problem is truly a research problem rather than merely a social or personal problem.

Whether the author of this proposal can avoid listing prehypotheses for hypothesis 2 depends on whether a committee can accept the statement that the evidence is "so well established" that no prehypotheses are needed. The references alone may be enough to satisfy a committee.

Hypotheses are generalizations; write them in present tense. Notice the wording, "children *are* better able to," and, "That greater understanding children *have* of." Do not write hypotheses as predictions; to do so disturbs the sense of a generalization or a statistical inference. A generalization is a claim that the data we observe apply generally—in the present hypothesis, "children *are* better able," not "*will be* able" in this one instance.

Note the reference to Piaget and Szeminska. This concludes a discussion of cardinality as that concept is learned by children. Consider the context of the research problem: How much do children of a certain age know about the concept of cardinality? Piaget and Szeminska were able to show the difficulty of the concept *quantity* and the distinctions within that concept. Committee members will want to know what test of cardinality fits with children's demonstrations of the concept.

gations for their cardinal values, while regarding the objects as undifferentiated (that is, one object has the same value as any other, and it makes no difference in what order the objects of a collection are called as long as each is called once). Likewise, when two sets are compared, each object is given an ordinal position (assigned an ordinal number—first, second, third, and so on) so that none is overlooked or counted twice. Sufficient care must be taken to count all objects only once if a correct quantity is given. The careful association of numbers to objects is a capacity that takes some time to develop.

Context of the Problem

The Scope of the Task When a Child Learns about Quantities

The more one examines the domain of theory about small numbers and lists those many number concepts that contribute to a child's competence with numbers, the more one comes to realize how complicated a small child's task is. Resnick (1986) has suggested a perspective that singles out two features: (a) In mathematics there are no objects to be noted; the knowledge is entirely abstract. When pointing to three objects, there is no number ''3'' that one can refer to. Moreover, Resnick said, concepts of number must be built without benefit of numbers to look at, or a number prototype. . . .

> This discussion should continue until the proposal has a complete rationale. Citations from the literature should form a history for the research problem and provide a logical basis for it. Choose only citations that fit concepts within the problem. Do not use citations merely to fill space.

Headings show how an introduction is organized. Note the headings opposite. Two levels are shown, a centered head ("Context of the Problem") and an elevated side head ("The Scope"). Had the discussion continued, one or more run-in paragraph heads could have been used for subordinate ideas. Notice the differences in capitalization, the underlining, and the absence of periods in the highest levels of headings. These heads conform to the rules in *Publication Manual of the American Psychological Association* (1983, p. 66).

"Context of the Problem" and "History of the Problem" are headings that fit research work better than the traditional "Literature Review." But they are better headings only if they provoke from a writer organized, relevant argument based on appropriate literature. The problem with "Literature Review" is that graduate students are prone to cite too freely rather than choosing from the literature only what fits a particular argument.

Experimentally Demonstrating a Child's Relative Understanding of Cardinal Number by Counting and by One-to-one Correspondence

I anticipate seating children at a table and confronting them with a succession of cardinality tasks that require them to (a) demon-

Make an operational problem statement. Here is a heading that begins "Experimentally Demonstrating." This section is intended as an operational expression of the problem. Be certain you understand clearly the purpose of an operational expression of a research problem (see Chapter 3,

strate equality, (b) demonstrate inequalities of both more and fewer, and (c) demonstrate transitivity. Each ability can be estimated separately when a child counts or uses one-to-one correspondence.

Counting. I will use cards having varying numbers of red dots in straight lines and, in the case of counting, will have children count blue poker chips they take from a pile and place in a bowl either to be equal to, or to be more numerous or fewer than, printed dots on the cards. I will then ask for *transitivity judgments* from the counting operations already performed (''If *a* > *b* and *b* > *c*, what is *a*'s relation to *c*?'').

Correspondence. To observe evidence of correspondence knowledge, I will use the same cards and poker chips as those used to make counting judgments. Children will take chips from a bowl and place those chips on a card next to red dots but not on top of them. Equalities, inequalities, *and transitivity* will be examined by correspondence.

p. 64). The operational expression has both expository and heuristic value; it helps make the problem clear and it shows how the abstract concept of the problem has been translated into physical research actions.

The physical actions here were chosen carefully to express the essence of the problem. The most central ideas in the statement are that children will place poker chips in rows in order to show equal rows, then one row fewer in number, and finally one row greater in number than the other. Clearly, the operations will be similar for counting and for one-to-one correspondence. That they are not *exactly* the same is important. The only detail needed is to give the statement a kind of narrative style or a simple, unambiguous form that all readers will understand. *Do not confuse an operational expression of a problem with the method of the study.* Though related, they serve entirely different purposes. The details that are appropriate for a method section are inappropriate here. Do not refer to numbers of subjects, their sexes, or other details that will detract from the conceptual heart of the problem. Look beyond the operations to the problem they are meant to represent. This operational statement is one of two expressions of the problem and should reveal exactly where the problem will be attacked. It is a reduction of the explanatory problem statement to the operations that confine the problem.

A PROPOSED METHOD

An example method is not shown here. Chapter 4, on writing a method section, demonstrates the content for method. Like introductions, method sections in proposals are similar to those in final reports and are not difficult to compose once a study has been designed.

Make some additions to your method section. To help your committee understand your study design, you should make some additions to the proposed method that students do not generally include. Create a heading at the end of the method section that reads, approximately, "How Data Will Be Displayed in My Thesis." Under this heading, create dummy tables and figures as you anticipate constructing them for the actual results in your thesis. Before each display, explain its purpose (for example, ''Table 1, which follows, shows how I will display my descriptive statistics: means, standard deviations, sample sizes, and so on. Notice that there are [a certain number] of [independent or classification variables], and note such and such, which explains the aspect of . . .''). Invent hypothetical data for your displays, showing results you might get.

CHAPTER 3

How to Write
a Research Introduction

This chapter tells how to write an introduction to a thesis or other research report. An introduction is the written expression of a research problem and its basis—nothing more. It is not reasonable to expect students to have a spontaneous ability to write problem statements. In fact, they seldom know what to say. To write a satisfactory introduction, you need a well-developed concept of a research problem. Your views of what a problem is will make a big difference in how quickly and how well you can do the writing. Chapter 2 prepared you for this chapter by emphasizing how you find or invent a research problem. It also enumerated the distinctive characteristics of research problems. *Master these problem characteristics as listed in Chapter 2.*

Suppose a graduate student has conceived a research problem and presented it in a thesis proposal. Later, when the student has analyzed all the data, he or she sits down to write the final report. Is the problem statement different in the final report? Very likely it is. Prepare yourself to think separately about the initial problem concept and the final one.

A DIFFERENCE IN RESEARCH PROBLEMS INVESTIGATED AND REPORTED

Naturally, a problem is probably not clearly understood when an investigator begins research. It is helpful to adopt the view that a research problem has two lives. Initially, a problem guides an investigator to evidence; then it undergoes a metamorphosis and emerges as an improved problem, to be expressed in a final report. Good scientists make these changes in a problem, and graduate students should do so as well.

First, you present a problem in a thesis proposal, and a professor asks for clarification. Later, the professor asks for revisions that improve the logic and replace vague concepts with specific ones. Eventually, a graduate committee tells you to proceed.

In the course of the study, as you come to see the problem in a more satisfactory way, you will express it differently. Of course, you will report those changes to your committee, and the committee will agree. In your final report, you should state your research problem in a way that takes advantage of what you learned in doing research.

A problem should be reported clearly in writing. However clear a problem may appear in the investigator's mind, it can be written vaguely. The most common reason for this vagueness is excessively general and abstract wording. Some writers write general problem statements in the misguided belief that a general expression sounds important, whereas a specific one sounds trivial. Your written exposition can succeed only if your problem statement is specific and limited to a manageable issue.

Problem statements you find in research literature may or may not be satisfactory. I once asked 14 students in a course in research writing to find problem statements in 15 articles selected by random number from 5 different American Psychological Association journals. Lines of print were numbered so that students could say that a problem begins at a given number and ends with another number. This made it possible to see to what degree the 14 students selected the same sentences as representing an author's intended research problem. There were wide differences in what the students identified as problem statements, so wide that sometimes the students had to infer from an entire article what its author might have intended as a problem.

When you express a research problem, use words that explicitly identify a passage as a research problem.   Fortunately, there were some articles in which all students did select the same passage as a problem statement. Usually the objective choice of a passage was provoked by a lead-in phrase like: "The problem we investigated was to . . ." Such problem-identifying phrases certainly helped students agree on the location of problems.

It is good practice to identify problem statements explicitly with words like:

1. The problem I investigated was _____.
2. This was a study of a relation between _____.
3. In this study I attempted to determine _____.
4. This is a report of two survey studies: (a) one to determine if _____ and (b) a second based on the first, to see how long it takes to _____.

Place these problem-identifying phrases at the very beginning of an introduction. When the problem statement is given first, a reader has a context for all that follows.

FOUR PARTS OF AN INTRODUCTION

An introduction can be complete and clear if it has four elements of exposition: (a) an explanatory expression—a statement that reveals a problem in certain relations among variables; (b) one or more suppositions suggesting a solution to the problem; (c) all of the presuppositions chosen as basis for each supposition; and (d) an operational expression of that same problem. When outlined, an introduction looks like this:

I. An *explanatory expression* of a problem that specifically identifies variables, *and includes:*
    A. A *supposition* that the variables identified hold a certain relation to each other
    B. *Presuppositions* to justify the supposition
II. An *operational expression* of that same problem

Both main elements, I and II, are problem statements; they are complementary and serve different purposes. The explanatory expression is the longer and more involved. It begins with explanation of certain very limited relations among variables. A supposition, more commonly called a *hypothesis,* should be part of an explanatory problem statement, as should the arguments for a supposition, known as *presuppositions.* Presuppositions should follow the particular supposition they support because you are, in effect, saying: "Here is a proposition, and now I must give you the arguments that make that proposition reasonable." A large part of an explanatory problem statement consists of these presuppositions or arguments.

Take time and give careful thought to explaining relations among variables. Your first efforts may not be satisfying, but you can improve and you can learn to organize your thinking and writing toward explaining phenomena. When you have data evidences with explanatory potential and have written your explanation, expect to revise your writing several times, with each revision more satisfactory than the last.

Your introduction should conclude with an operational expression of the problem. This expression describes concretely what you as an investigator did, and thereby it reveals what particular aspect of the larger problem has been attacked. Operational expressions are carefully chosen physical transactions that reveal research strategy.

Example of a Written Introduction Containing the Four Elements of a Research Problem

To illustrate the content and order of presentation in an introduction to a research report, a reconstruction follows from the famous mother surrogate studies by Harry F. Harlow (1971). Those studies by Harlow illustrate the development of theory to explain behavior. A student who wants a guide for writing research problems, one that explains the basis for suppositions and demonstrates effective expression of the ideas, will do well to study Professor Harlow's book *Learning to Love* (1971).

The emphasis in Harlow's research is on explanation. In the present case, Professor Harlow was interested in identifying one or more principal variables that account for an infant's emotional attachment to its mother. By the time Harlow had completed his research, he was able to say with confidence what is important for infant attachment to a mother.

The example is intended as the first words and paragraphs of an introduction to a research report (a thesis or a journal article). To create a suitable illustration of a thesis introduction, short quotations have been taken from pages 5 through 18 of *Learning to Love* (1971). These quotations have been placed in a different order from Harlow's to illustrate the four main elements in a research problem and show how these four elements might appear in an introduction to a thesis. Although the words are mainly Professor Harlow's, I have joined some paragraphs by a few words of my own (underlined to represent italics) to coordinate the paragraphs.

Note, in particular, that the headings are *not* Professor Harlow's. These headings were created here to demonstrate to you how to use headings to organize a thesis introduction and to make the main points of logic for a problem. Now, turn your attention to Professor Harlow's arguments explaining infant monkeys' emotional attachments to their mothers.

AN EXAMPLE INTRODUCTION*

In this study I attempted to determine if physical contact between a mother and her infant
monkey is a strong basis for emotional attachment of an infant to its mother. Early indications in this work appeared to lend weight to my
supposition that ''a primary function or obliga-
tion of the monkey mother is to provide her infant with intimate bodily contact, which is the
basic mechanism in eliciting love from the neonate and infant'' (Harlow, 1971, p. 7).

Although infant monkeys are dependent on
their mothers for nourishment and protection,
the supposition that I tested was that bodily
contact between mother and infant is relatively
more powerful than other variables in bonding an
infant to its mother; in particular, surface
contact is more powerful than a mother's offering of milk to satisfy an infant's hunger.

On the other hand, some ''psychologists
and psychoanalysts have long assumed that the
infant's love for the mother developed through
association of the mother with organic pleasures
resulting from the ingestion of milk and the alleviation of hunger. According to this 'cupboard
theory' of infant love, as Bowlby (1969) has
termed it, the fundamental mechanisms are those
related to functions of the breast'' (p. 17).

''Psychologists and their social science
allies had long thought that mother love was a
derived drive which developed from the associations of the mother image with the alleviation
of the primary drive of hunger. Motivation theory was dominated by the thesis that the only
important unlearned motives were such homeo-
static biological drives as hunger, thirst,
elimination, and organic sex. All other motives
were considered derived, learned, or secondary''
(p. 18).

What to notice in the example. Notice that the very first sentence declares a purpose, "to determine if." Explicit statements of purpose are helpful to readers. Pay special attention to the fact that the first paragraph, as it should, gets right into the problem, with no preliminaries and no attempt to build a broad general context. Readers of research want to get quickly to the heart of the problem.

An explanatory expression. Continuing from the first paragraph through the presuppositions is an explanatory expression of the problem. Scan this explanatory expression, stopping at the heading "Operations to Separate the Confounded Variables."

Suppositions (hypotheses) in the first and second paragraphs. The supposition in paragraph 1 is a preliminary one, ("Early indications") followed in paragraph 2 by the supposition actually tested in the research. Whether or not you express a similar change in suppositions in your writing to show the progress of your thinking, you should at least embed the best developed supposition someplace in your explanatory expression. Because suppositions are effective devices for directing a reader's thinking and for organizing the ideas that follow, they are best placed early in the explanatory expression.

In this third paragraph is a countersupposition, one that competes with the investigator's. Not all theorists have countersuppositions competing with their own. Harlow's research was a direct challenge to this countersupposition.

Headings. Notice the amount of information in the headings. Usually, the most essential ideas on a page are given in headings, just as a presupposition is given here in the next heading. Give the complete idea; don't simply hint.

---

*This section is adapted with the publisher's permission from *Learning to Love* by H. F. Harlow. Copyright 1971, Albion Publishing Company, San Francisco.

Although the supposition was not given in a heading, it could have been done and might have been more effective. Consider creating a heading for your supposition.

A Presupposition that Innate Sex Differences Prepare a Female for Motherhood

''Behavioral differences between the sexes have often been attributed entirely to learning and culture. Learning is no doubt a factor of considerable significance, particularly in human beings, but there are also far more subtle, secretive, inborn variables. By the time children are four or five years old they show awareness of sex-appropriate behavior which appears to be determined by a combination of genetic factors and experience (Gari and Scheinfeld, 1968)'' (p. 5).

''Sex differences in nonhuman primates cannot be explained simply in terms of learned variables. There is reason to believe that genetic variables condition similar differences in human primates. The gentle and relatively passive behavior characteristic of most little girls is a useful maternal attribute, and the more aggressive behavior of most little boys is useful preparation for the paternal function of protection'' (pp. 5, 6).

''In addition to differences in general personality traits, there are sex differences more directly related to motherhood. Girls will respond to babies—all babies—long before they approach adolescence'' (p. 6).

Differences between Female and Male Monkeys in Their Affective Responses to Infants

''Attitude differences that are apparently inherent were demonstrated in the responses of preadolescent female and male macaque monkeys to rhesus monkey babies (Chamove, Harlow, and Mitchell, 1967). Since the preadolescent macaques had never seen infants younger than themselves and had not been raised by real monkey mothers who could have imparted their own attitudes toward babies, we may assume that the differences in response pattern were primarily innately determined'' (p. 6).

''When they were confronted with a baby monkey, almost all the responses made by the female monkeys were positive and pleasant, including contact, caressing, and cuddling. These mat-

Presuppositions. One or more presuppositions are absolutely essential to a supposition. If you express a supposition you must also express at least one presupposition that led you to the supposition. Wherever you are now, you must have come from someplace, and your reader wants to know where. Because one of Professor Harlow's suppositions was that surface contact is more powerful than a mother's milk in attracting an infant, readers can ask for the basis of that supposition. The basis is the presuppositions.

Notice, in the opposite text, how Harlow's presupposition has been developed to show that learning alone cannot explain these sex differences. Then, just before the next heading, he said, "Girls will respond to babies—all babies—long before they approach adolescence" (p. 6). Further on, when referring to monkeys he said, "the female monkeys were positive and pleasant, including contact, caressing, and cuddling" (p. 6).

Harlow was preparing a basis for saying that females are innately prepared for surface attraction to their infants. Remember, however, that Harlow's supposition is about an infant's attraction to a mother, not a mother's attraction to an infant. But if the attraction is to continue, it must be reciprocal. An infant cannot pursue an unresponsive mother—hence the foundation of his argument that female attraction to infants is innate.

Understandable headings. To be understandable, headings usually should be longer and should include prepositions. Often, students write headings that are too cryptic to convey the intended ideas.

The headings opposite were constructed with careful thought to containing central information, so that the paragraphs that follow them simply need to fill in the detail of the arguments. For help in

ernal-type baby responses were conspicuously absent in the males. Instead the male monkeys exhibited threatening and aggressive behavior toward the babies, although fortunately this behavior never progressed to the point of real physical abuse or injury'' (p. 6).

The Rapid Development in Female Monkeys of Affection for Infants and the Subsequent Restriction of That Affection to the Mother's Own Offspring

''During the infant monkey's first week of life maternal love is indiscriminate, and during this period a monkey mother will respond with equal intensity to her own or to a strange infant of similar age. Earlier research had indicated that mothers are very upset by separation from their infants, but that their distress is somewhat allayed when they can see the infants. However, a more recent experiment (Jensen, 1965) demonstrates that they are relieved by the sight of *any* infant until their own offspring are a week to ten days old. After that point only the sight of their own infants will satisfy them. Evidently a monkey mother develops feelings specific to her own infant only after she has interacted with it for a period of time'' (p. 9).

A Presupposition That Female Primates Are Specially Prepared by Skin Sensitivity for Nurturing Skin Contact with Their Infants

''Recent research efforts have been directed toward examining sex differences in human newborns, differences that occur so early they cannot be attributed to learning. . . . Newborn females seem to be more responsive to skin exposure. They react more strenuously than newborn males to a covering blanket, are more disturbed when their skin is stimulated by an air jet, and are higher in basal skin conductance (Hamburg and Lunde, 1966)'' (p. 5).
''For almost all monkey mothers the initial appearance of the infant releases love, as evidenced by positive and spontaneous approach and cradling responses. During the first month of life the mother maintains her baby either in a close ventral-ventral position [. . .] or in a looser and more relaxed cradling posture in which the infant's body is held gently within the confines of the mother's arms and legs. This position provides the maximum amount of bodily contact between mother and infant. Such physical

creating a correctly subordinated series of headings, consult a style manual like the *Publication Manual of the American Psychological Association,* third edition (1983), p. 65; also see Chapter 7 of this book.

Continued explanation. In this paragraph, notice the succession of ideas. Here, Professor Harlow carried forward the concept of an innate preparation of females for motherhood and capped his claim with evidence that the innate preference for any infant undergoes a transition, with monkey mothers becoming selective toward their own offspring. This paragraph, along with the others, exemplifies what is meant by an *explanatory expression.* The explanation, however, is not entirely evident until you take the set of presuppositions together with the supposition they support.

Another presupposition. This presupposition is directly foundational for a supposition that contact comfort will overpower nursing as a basis for infant attachment to a mother. You might prefer to have this presupposition precede the one that argues that females have innate specialized responses to infants. However, you can see that the preceding presupposition prepares for this one about skin sensitivity. Two defining characteristics of presuppositions are that (a) a presupposition is never the same proposition as the supposition it supports, although they always have related elements, and (b) a presupposition always contains a basis for believing the supposition it supports, though not necessarily a sufficient basis. Several presuppositions taken together make a supposition more believable than any single presupposition.
Notice the argumentative nature of the passage. The topic sentence appears first, followed by the specific empirical basis for it: ''During the first week of life . . .''

attachments seem to be comforting for both mother and infant, an observation that has given rise to the concept of contact comfort. The monkey mother both gives and receives contact comfort, and it may be assumed that contact is an important mechanism in eliciting maternal love from the mother'' (pp. 7, 8).

''The role of infant body contact, clinging, and nursing in eliciting maternal love was demonstrated some years ago at the Wisconsin Primate Laboratories. One monkey mother was separated from her infant and allowed to adopt a young kitten. Initially the monkey mother made every effort to mother the kitten, even to the point of initiating nursing. However, the kitten exhibited one enormous behavioral flaw; it could not cling to the mother's body. When the kitten failed to reciprocate the mother's contact-clinging efforts, monkey maternal love waned, and after 12 days the kitten was totally abandoned'' (p. 8).

''In a recent experiment (Deets, 1969) four monkey mothers were given the opportunity to adopt 'twins,' two newborns, neither of which was the mother's own infant [. . .]. All four mothers at first attempted to initiate ventral contact and suckling with their infants. However, the twin infants, clinging in a haphazard way to themselves as well as to the mother, did not provide the kind of clinging and suckling feedback that is maximally reinforcing for the mother monkey'' (p. 8).

''The mothers experienced great difficulty in establishing a satisfactory contact-clinging relationship, and three of the four mothers became ambivalent toward their twin infants and began to alternately accept and reject each. While the mothers eventually did accept the twins totally and permanently, affectional ambivalence continued for as long as a month in one case. Similar ambivalence was demonstrated by a monkey who gave birth to a pair of natural twins in our laboratory'' (pp. 8, 9).

Two Naturally Confounded Factors in Mother–Infant Affection

Affection of Infant for Mother and Mother for Infant Is Naturally Confounded

''Infant love, which is the love of the neonate, baby, and young child for the mother, has often been confused with maternal love. These two affectional systems, the mother's love

These details of argument show the investigator's integration of his own work with that of other investigators and, to some degree, mastery of the interrelated workings of variables relevant to infant attachment. The literature you cite should be similarly interwoven with your own work to show some understanding of the variables you have studied. Dissertations that have a separate section called "Literature review" are all too often disjointed, rambling discourses. If your mentors agree, place closely relevant literature together with your expression of the problem in a way that integrates it with your own observations and interpretations.

Presuppositions originate in various ways, including semiformal or even informal observations. Notice the argumentative value of Harlow's reference to "one monkey mother [that] was separated from her infant." Careful investigators make notes of events that may be helpful in writing a research report. Even relatively pure analytical concepts are part of the presuppositional logic. This logic is not limited to experimental research. It is just as much a part of descriptive research if that research is to contribute to a reader's beliefs about the phenomena studied.

The report writer's judgment determines how many explicit statements of presuppositions are needed. In this illustration there are only two, and this small number makes organization of the example simple. As you will note across the page, however, there are presuppositions that are not separately identified. One might write: I have identified "A Presupposition That Monkey Mothers Manifest Frustration When They Are Unable to Cuddle Twins Simultaneously." This presupposition is another form of argument that the contact comfort shared between mother and infant has a strong basis.

Confounded factors. This section has an important place in this introduction. The discussion is preparation for an operational expression of the research problem describing how the confounded variables have been disentangled in the study. One paragraph tells how

for the infant and the infant's love for the mother, operate simultaneously and are difficult to separate and unravel under normal physical and developmental circumstances. The intimate physical proximity and the close reciprocal relationship between mothers and infants make it difficult to distinguish the variables producing maternal affection for the baby from those producing baby affection for the mother. For example, nursing is an important variable in both affectional systems, but it is impossible under normal circumstances to determine its relative contribution to each. However, this does not mean that the mechanisms underlying each kind of love cannot be analyzed separately'' (p. 17).

Infant's Attraction to Mother's Milk and to Surface Contact with Her Are Naturally Confounded

Distinguishing between an infant's motivation for a mother's milk and its motivation for physical contact with her is difficult. ''Infantile satisfaction of hunger and thirst is essentially guaranteed from the monkey mother by the pattern of body-to-body and breast-to-breast ventral-ventral positioning. The neonatal monkey is held tightly by the monkey mother, with its mouth at or near the level of the mother's breasts. Infantile attachments to the breast in both human and monkey infants are also facilitated by rooting reflexes, which are head-turning responses to cheek stimulation, and subsequent nipple attachment and suckling. Each monkey infant has an almost exclusive preference for one breast over the other; however, half the infants prefer the left breast and half prefer the right, demonstrating complete statistical impartiality'' (pp. 9, 10).

Operations to Separate the Confounded Variables

To separate the confounded variables, ''Harlow (1958) constructed sets of nursing and non-nursing cloth and wire surrogate mothers. One primary variable differentiating the two types of surrogate mothers was that of body surface. The wire surrogates had bare bodies of welded wire and the cloth surrogates were covered by soft, resilient terrycloth sheaths. The two surrogates . . . had long, tapered bodies which could be easily clasped by the infant rhe-

the dependent variable "emotional attachment" is confounded in nature; an observer cannot tell whether he or she is observing mother attachment or infant attachment. The next paragraph tells how the independent variables of nursing and surface contact are confounded in the mother's body. It follows that these variables must be experimentally separated to satisfy a supposition that surface contact has greater attraction for an infant than food.

The smooth transition from an explanatory expression of a problem to an operational expression, such as you see developing here, is not always so easy to achieve. View the transition in this way: First there is a problem explained, which terminates with reference to confounded variables; next, the problem appears as operations that solve the confounding of variables. Think of operational expressions of research problems as solutions (the operations that resolve the problem). Professor Harlow's research solution to the problem made a logical transition from problem to solution relatively easy to write.

How detailed should your argument be? How much detail you need is a matter of judgment. Include complete ideas, sufficient to explain and interpret your problem. In this example one might include a discussion of inferences applied to living animals when artificial animals are used in experimentation. How valid, for example, are the inferences made by Lorenz, Hess, and Thompson when they used artificial birds in studying the imprinting of baby birds to their mothers?

An operational expression of the problem. An operational expression of a problem is the problem expressed concretely as physical operations. Such a problem statement serves a very important expository purpose; it exposes the specific attack the investigator made on the problem. Notice how much information is provided to a reader here. Up to this point, the general problem is clear, but there is no suggestion of a method for attacking it. The problem statement opposite limits the problem to only those variable relations

sus monkey. Some of the surrogates were endowed with a single breast, and some had none (the nursing surrogate mothers did not need two breasts, since none ever gave birth to twins)'' (p. 18, 19).

''A cloth mother and a wire mother were set up in a cubicle attached to the baby's living cage. For four newborn monkeys the cloth mothers lactated and the wire mothers did not; for four other monkey infants this condition was reversed. In both situations the infant received all its milk from the appropriate surrogate breast as soon as it was able to sustain itself in this manner'' (p. 19).

To provide evidence of infant attachment to one of the surrogates (the dependent variables, I counted the frequency of infant retreats to each mother surrogate when an infant was frightened and measured the duration of time spent on her.

that are expressed as operations and as tangible apparatus.

Independent variables are identified in the next to last paragraph. Be careful to choose the right words for an operational expression of a problem. Including operational details here will only detract from the revelation of the problem. Your purpose here is not an exposition of method; leave that for the method section, which has a very different purpose. Here, words and sentences are needed that reveal how an investigator *limited the operations* or *selected the point among the variables* at which to attack the problem. Harlow limited his problem to operations that compare nursing to surface contact for their relative contributions to an infant's attachment to a mother. There are, of course, other aspects of infant attachment he did not choose to study. Investigators must always make such choices.

Dependent variables have been identified here as the frequency with which an infant retreated to a mother when frightened and the duration of an infant's stay on the mother. You might fill out the statement a little more by beginning, ''Infants were allowed access to a mother surrogate'' and ending, ''and certain other criteria were taken as evidence of the infant monkey's affective response to surface contact and to a nursing bottle.''

REDUCING A PROBLEM TO A WRITTEN STATEMENT

Begin your introduction with an explanatory expression of your problem. Limit your use of general, abstract expressions. Look back at the first paragraph of the Harlow example to see how concretely and specifically it begins. In the case of Harlow's investigations, suppose the written expression of the problem were excessively abstract and general, even though the research operations remained the same. There might be an opening statement like this:

Mothers manifest great affection for their infants, and infants appear to acquire specific affective responses to their mothers. Some theorists have called this attachment ''bonding'' (Jones, 1930 [fictitious]). These theorists have placed importance on the concept of bonding, saying that normal social and emotional adjustment is dependent on it [citation]. If bonding is real, what is its basis?

The foregoing illustrates an abstract beginning that hints at what could turn out to be any one of a large number of research questions. *No research problem has been developed in the statement to this point.* If these four sentences are to be the first ones in an introduction, a writer should shift quickly to reduce these concepts to whatever is problematic in that research. Unless a writer is more specific, readers cannot tell whether the study is about aberrant social adjustment in children, about the various manifestations of maternal affection, about recip-rocated acts between mothers and their infants, or about some other phenom-enon. Too much abstraction not only is unnecessary in exposing a research prob-lem; it actually impedes readers' comprehension. Express only those abstractions that play a part in explaining *relevant phenomena.* Even these referents should be tied to concrete representations. Pause long enough here to look in Chapter 7 at the section headed: "Explain, Don't Simply Label." That section will help you avoid excessively abstract language.

Consider the concept of *levels of abstraction.* The highest levels are thor-oughly abstract and general; the lowest are both tangible and specific. Both the abstract and the concrete or tangible play an important part in written exposition, but in writing problem statements the concrete needs emphasis because writers tend to be too abstract. Figure 3.1 is a schematic representation of research prob-lems at three levels of abstraction. The most abstract, level 3, may be where most investigators begin thinking before they plan their research and before they have any data.

For example, we don't know what Harlow's first question was—perhaps, simply, "What is the basis for infants' attachment?" Such a preinvestigation question is represented at level 3 in the upper right of Figure 3.1. It is a level 3 problem, a problem not yet developed for research. Level 3 problems are thor-oughly abstract, open, and general. Because they are too general, level 3 prob-lems are not directly answerable. The statement suggests no solution to the prob-lem, as it would if an independent variable were named in the statement to explain infants' attachment to a mother.

With careful thought and many observations, however, an investigator may understand certain relations between variables and be ready to express a problem in the form it should take for a thesis or a journal article. Abstraction level 2, an explanatory problem statement, is best for expressing these relations among variables. Such an expression is more explicit and specific than level 3.

Notice that although such a statement explicitly identifies relations among variables, a level 2 problem is *not directly answerable.* An expression at this inter-mediate level of generality must be reduced to a level 1 expression before readers know what ramification of the problem was studied. At level 1, an operational expression of a problem is *directly answerable* because there is only one set of concrete, specific research operations, those actually carried out in the study. Any generalizations and inferences are drawn from and limited by these specific operations. The general expression written at level 2 is the conceptual source for the physical transactions at level 1, the actual research operations of an investiga-tor. Level 1, therefore, refers to the same problem as level 2, except that level 1 is a written expression of only one ramification of level 2.

Suppositions should be expressed in the intermediate range of specificity (level 2) when they have relatively general application. They should be expressed specifically (level 1) when they refer to specific research operations.

A final point about Figure 3.1: It is meant to demonstrate a reason for expressing a research problem in two ways, as *explanation* of a supposition or hypothesis and as *operations.* To understand a problem, readers must know the

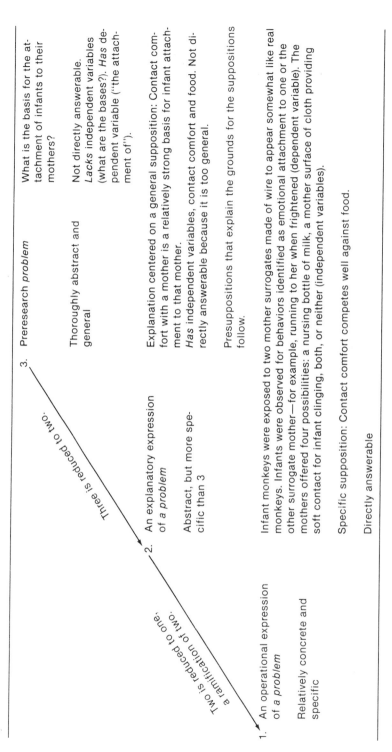

FIGURE 3.1. Ideational content of a problem expressed at three levels of abstraction. Level 3 is an expression at an early stage of investigation. Levels 2 and 1 are postinvestigative expressions, expressions appropriate for research reporting. Level 2 is a reduction of the abstractions at level 3. Level 1 is a further reduction from level 2 and is a specific ramification of level 2.

place in some field of knowledge where a study was directed (level 2) and the limits of that study (level 1). The physical operations identify the concrete phenomena to which the study is limited. No study can be conducted at level 2; in other words, no study can possibly respond to all the specific instances in the general proposition or explanatory expression. An operational expression is one ramification; it is one of those studies.

AN EXPLANATORY EXPRESSION OF A PROBLEM

One way to give a problem context is to state, at some point in a theory, a problem that will put the theory to test. Such a statement pulls in related aspects of the theory to build a rationale for the study. Consider the following two expressions as problem statements. Both are meant to be the very first words of a thesis. Notice that both immediately get at a problem, and both are specific; the first, however, has more theoretical context. (Note that this is a hypothetical problem, not H. F. Harlow's.)

> In my study of emotional attachment of infant to mother, I set about to get evidence for a proposition that satisfaction of an infant's hunger by a mother is basis for the infant's emotional attachment. I reasoned that the cathexis of infant to mother comes about when the suckling response is satisfied by a mother's milk and sucking is accompanied by emotions of satisfaction. Such emotions are a secondary response—response association to food in the stomach.

One need not share a belief in such a theory to see the writer's intention to explain a problem. Because the explanation is not complete, with all the evidence for the writer's position, the writer will go on to reveal the presuppositions (arguments and evidence) on which nursing was taken as basis for infant attachment.

An investigator-writer shows skill as a research scientist when a theory appears vulnerable to the research operations that were carried out; the theory is really susceptible to testing in the study. The reporting rhetoric will then demonstrate to a reader that the investigator knew how to get convincing evidence. Moreover, much of the persuasiveness lies in the completeness and clarity of the theoretical relations expressed in the written statement.

Now, examine another theory meant to explain the same dependent variable, infant attachment. (This is a reconstruction of the work by H. F. Harlow.)

> Coincidental to the present study, my colleagues and I observed macaque monkeys over several months. During that time we noticed the infant monkeys' strong liking for contact with things soft, comfortable, and warm. We have come to call that preference "contact comfort," and have supposed that such contact plays a great part in the infants' attachment to a soft mother. As yet, we can offer no mechanism to account for such a preference but have been interested in demonstrating its strength.

> Since there exists a general belief that familial attachment of infants to their mothers results from the mother's instrumentality in satisfying an infant's basic physical needs (i.e., for food) we did our investigation to test the infant's relative preference for a mother's milk or a mother's soft contact. We began our study believing that contact comfort might hold its own against food.

As far as this second expression goes, the problem statement has little explanatory content—only a supposed link between softness of physical contact and attachment to mother. But minor linkages may be all you are confident of at the time, and these minor linkages do set a problem in context.

Explanatory expressions of research problems are indications of heuristic progress; ideally, they show an investigator's success in explaining some phenomenon. The more explanation based on evidence you can offer, the more complete will be your rationale. Said differently, an explanatory expression of a problem not only reveals what an investigator knows and doesn't know, but also reveals existing facts and established beliefs of other thinkers.

Empirical Questions: Questions Not Based in Theory or Supposition

Questions with no explanatory basis are *empirical* questions. They have no value in a research report because they do not inform. Two-tailed statistical questions and other questions for which you have no hunches are empirical questions. A question like, "I wonder what is under that rock?" is an empirical question if it can be answered by picking up the rock and looking. Empirical questions are separated from explanatory questions by the amount of reasoning and evidence you must have for an explanatory question (the amount of theory behind the question).

Empirical questions that remain so after investigation and to which you can add little structure and cannot create an explanatory context are not of much interest. Research analysts and journal editors turn away from such questions because they fail to contribute importantly to what we know. The general assumption is that research is carried out to form explanations, or at least to create hypothetical relations (structure) by which to understand phenomena. With empirical questions, one expects to make progress so that after research is completed, it will be possible to give at least some minimal structure to the question. Such structure has been called here "an explanatory expression of the problem." In practice, the amount of structure (explanation or theory) will vary widely from one study to another, but you should express some structure by the time your research is ready for reporting.

Do not form the impression that an explanation of any quality or of whimsical origin is satisfactory. If your research and thinking have failed to produce reasonably good explanations and suppositions, then forcing their creation is worse than useless. Time is needed to acquire ideas and more time to think through them. The quality of that thinking is what will make you a good investigator and report writer.

In perspective, empirical questions are important in research strategy and conducting research, but they are only incidental in writing a report of research. Most research probably passes through a series of empirical questions where the succession gives evidence of progress in an investigator's thinking.

An Example of Failure to Create an Explanatory Research Problem

The two-paragraph statement that follows was invented for you to consider. What was the author's aim? Where in the text is an explanatory expression of a problem? Finally, how do you classify the statement?

Investigators of school learning have generally neglected a search for variables that are controllable and which influence school achievement. Smith (1979) classified 1,325 published studies, finding that only 0.08 of them reported on variables that are controllable (can be manipulated) and that influence school learning. According to Jones (1985) and Brown (1971), researchers have been preoccupied with correlates of achievement that are not controllable. Such variables include classification variables like sex, age, race, and the like, which have often been studied for their relations to other variables, and much is now known about such relationships. Moreover, aptitude variables have also been investigated from as many perspectives as humans think to fit to their formulas.

We have been interested in identifying a variable that can be manipulated and that might influence reading comprehension. Time spent at a task is a variable that may influence comprehension, and time can be deliberately varied. We therefore set about measuring recall of units of information according to time elapsed since readers began reading. We wanted to know if the acquisition of information occurs at a constant rate as reading time passes. If not, then reading periods should be regulated in length so as to yield the maximum amount of learning.

Analyzing the Statement

What was the author's aim? In the first paragraph, it was to show that the author has good values. There is *no research problem* (no relevant explanation) in either paragraph. The first paragraph is a little homily about neglect—neglect of practical research by other researchers or, more particularly, research not aimed at control of variables. The author may not have known how to begin the report and so impulsively started with a pet grievance or with the first idea that came to mind.

Occasionally, students believe they must justify their research by arguing how their research can be applied. Research justifies itself by what it permits us to report confidently, clearly, and precisely, not by its central place in the universe. Never refer to your own topic as *vital, crucial,* or even *important;* the world's skeptics will be alerted. What you may call important never makes of it a research problem. Words like *critical* and *crucial* belong in hospital emergency rooms; they never fit comfortably in research reports. Temperate, unexaggerated expressions win sympathetic eyes.

Use the introduction to reveal a problem and its context. Explain relationships between variables. Use language that is temperate, unexaggerated, and free of value statements and exhortations.

In the second paragraph of this fictitious research problem, one good thing is that two variables are named—*time on task,* which apparently is an independent variable, and *reading comprehension,* a dependent variable. If the variables in the second paragraph are related functionally, then the evidence is likely to show that reading comprehension varies as reading time progresses (comprehension is functionally dependent on the time a reader has been at the task of reading). All studies must involve variables, but not all studies examine functional relations (one variable causes the other).

Paragraph 2 contains only an empirical question. It has no explanatory content to suggest why amount remembered should vary with the length of time one has been reading. Not even a minor theoretical link is suggested. The question is classified in statistical theory as a two-tailed question: Either (a) the rate of comprehension will decrease as time passes, or (b) the rate will increase as time passes. Moreover, comprehension might not relate in any way to time spent reading.

It would have been easy to express the problem as a one-tailed problem—for example, "We wanted to know if the acquisition of information decreases as readers continue to read." Does this transform the statement into an explanatory expression? No, it remains an empirical question. The problem now implies that comprehension suffers with the passage of time, but there is no suggestion as to why it should suffer. Telling *why* comprehension might suffer will transform the statement into an explanatory expression of the problem. For example, suppose you were to suggest that fatigue is a likely factor in degrading comprehension. Then there is the suggestion of a theory. To create a theory that explains, however, you must reveal the relations that show how comprehension varies with changes in fatigue.

WRITING AN EXPLANATORY PROBLEM STATEMENT

No one can write completely satisfactory thesis problems. Research problems are not like mathematics problems with simple objective qualities; mathematic problems can be called *well structured* because they have exact elements leading to just one unambiguous outcome. Logicians refer to *well-structured problems* and to *ill-structured problems* in theories of problem solving and artificial intelligence (Reitman, 1964; Simon, 1973). By those classifications, even the more satisfactory problems in research literature tend to be ill structured. Although no one can show you how to write well-structured research problems, we can identify correct content for the statements.

Explanatory Expressions of Problems in Descriptive Research

Explanatory expressions are needed in all research, regardless of topic or method. All descriptive research requires a problem statement that explains the reason for the study. The word *explanatory* has the same general meaning for descriptive research as for other kinds. All research problems are explanations of something; without explanation, the research will appear trivial because it is trivial. If, for example, an investigator has intercorrelated seven variables, then a problem statement must say *why* these variables were analyzed as intercorrelations.

There is no research problem in a statement that simply says, "In this study I set out to determine the intercorrelations among seven variables." An investigator must have had expectations when the study was begun; if the study was well thought out, there were good reasons to look for correlations among certain of the variables.

An explanatory problem statement should include content like the following examples and should be expressed in similar language (identify all variables):

1. I set out to find whether variable X is directly related to Y above a scale value of $X = 25$. Such a relation is probably weak but positive because (a), (b), (c) . . .

2. This was a study of phenomenon A, often observed by others [citation]. The problem we [multiple investigators] undertook was to see if by X [independent variable], we could effect Y [dependent variable]. We chose to represent X at three levels because at those values, Y should be most vulnerable to influence. Among all the influences on Y, X should be among the greatest because [some logical joining of the variables]. Then, too, the three levels of X were selected because at these junctures, _____.

3. In this study, I attempted to find a way to produce _____ having qualities (a), (b), (c), and (d). To get (a), it is necessary to do _____; to get (b) _____; to get quality (c) has always been a two-step process: _____ and _____. There are few suggestions in literature on getting (d), but I reasoned that if I were to _____, (d) might result.

   It was my belief that if all qualities (a) through (d) can be obtained together, then Y will be a more satisfactory state because _____. Since the ordinary scale values of Y range from Y to Y', I had hope of extending those values to Y''. In this report, I have related my successive experiences in developing (a) through (d) and also an incidental discovery of yet another influence on Y, previously unreported.

The significance and meaning of the correlations is the explanatory content of the problem statement. A correlation between plant growth and the amount of sunlight a plant receives is only an empirical fact. Explanations of why the relation holds are based in plant physiology; an investigator should express the problem in whatever physiological terms will explain the plant's dependence on sunlight for its growth.

An Example of an Explanatory Expression in Survey Research

The following is a fictional problem statement that is not very different from some seen in education and other social enterprises where administrative theory is studied. The example illustrates how a rationale can be expressed in the first paragraphs of an introduction.

Efficiency of management depends on how quickly action is taken to complete an administrative task. This was a survey study of administrators' quickness of response to new tasks. For the survey data reported here, I formed questions provoked by this rationale: School and hospital officials derive tasks from other persons' initiatives and from their own. These initiatives are of two classes, ones that can be satisfied quickly (i.e., by writing a letter, by making a brief inquiry, or by giving instructions to an assistant), and initiatives that require thought and extensive action.

My hypothesis was that those persons requiring the fewest steps to resolve simple initiatives have more systematic schemes for attacking complex initiatives.

Officials who can despatch simple initiatives in the fewest steps will have more time to resolve complex initiatives and to consider philosophical aspects of running organizations. Wilson and Smith (1992) have shown that managers who resolve simple tasks quickly are more analytical than other managers. In a previous study of my own, I found that quick resolution of simple tasks positively associates with the amount of time a manager spends by himself in his office (Smith, 1988). There is reason to think that quiet time is devoted to the solution of complex problems.

The purpose of the survey was to obtain normative data showing how many steps administrators require to resolve simple initiatives, and to relate the number of these steps to modes of attack that administrators use in working on complex initiatives. The data on complex initiatives have been compared, in the present study, to an idealized schedule of solutions to arrive at an index of efficiency. It was then possible to relate indexes of efficiency to years of experience in administration and to other contemporaneous variables.

In analyzing modes of attack on complex initiatives, I first divided tasks into three groups as follows: (a) those tasks that do not require the approval or assistance of others, (b) those tasks that require the approval or assistance of no more than two other persons, and (c) those tasks that require the approval of a board or the assistance of more than two other persons. From this point, I used Jones (1989), "Schedule of Transactions Required to Complete Administrative Tasks," to classify my respondents' modes of attack on complex initiatives.

Notice that the explanatory expression of a problem for this survey research is based in a simple rationale. Readers can see the purpose from an explanatory problem statement.

Be patient with this long chapter and its ramifications. True, this entire chapter is about writing a short introduction. However, mastery of its concepts will allow you to write with more confidence.

An Example of an Explanatory Expression of a Problem in Educational Research and Development

This following research problem suffers from its lack of a real origin, but it illustrates the language of explanation in problem statements. The very first words of an introduction should get right at a problem, as in this example.

This was a study of children's natural language, which I carried out as part of my preparation for writing a series of children's readers. I reasoned that I should base the language of the readers on (a) the kinds of words and short sentences children actually use, and (b) the kinds of purposes and motives children commonly express.

To accomplish that, I collected a large body of natural sentences of children. Those sentences were classified according to the frequency of their occurrence in children's ordinary language and according to the purposes the sentences represented. The classifications were based on Smith's (1989) scheme of "progressive sentence formation," and Black's (1983, 1991, 1994) studies of motives evident in children's language.

According to Smith, children's sentences can be ordered in six successive categories that accompany language development. I have attempted to identify motivational elements in Smith's six progressive types of sentences that correspond to motives Black revealed in her studies. These corresponding motives seemed likely to provide topics for the readers that will interest children. The motivational elements fit two broad categories: (a) fantasy and (b) children's real-life episodes. Black (1981) has given two lines of analysis for extracting children's interests from their expressed motivation. These are . . .

Whatever the subject of the research, a problem statement needs to have explanatory content. In problems of pure science, the theoretical content is a more obvious necessity than in some other kinds of research. Unfortunately, even in pure science, it is quite possible to express only an empirical question without giving any reason for asking it.

An explanatory expression of a problem is needed in every research report, regardless of the research method or the philosophy of discovery. *All* explanatory problem statements *include* (a) references to variables, (b) at least one supposition (hypothesis), and (c) several presuppositions (prehypotheses) for each supposition.

SUPPOSITIONS

A supposition (hypothesis) is a supposed relation between variables. A supposition may be expressed as in the following: "We interpreted the studies by [so and so] together with our own observations of _____ to justify a supposition that whenever A appears, B is present."

When an investigator thinks he or she has recognized (discovered) a possible relation between variables, the expression of the relation is called a supposition. The term *supposition* means that the relation is hypothetical (unproved and probably unprovable in an absolute sense). In effect, an investigator says: "B appears always to be an accompaniment of A. I wonder if B really does always accompany A." With sufficient observation and thinking, that investigator may develop an unshakable confidence in the relation, but such propositions remain hypothetical because ordinarily there is no way to test the full range of possibilities.

Because all hypotheses are suppositions, and vice versa, you may use either term in writing, but do not switch back and forth in the same article. *Hypothesis* is a more widely understood term.

Suppositions do not differ from hypotheses. In research reports, the word *hypothesis* is more common. In philosophy of science, the words *hypothesis* and *supposition* have been used interchangeably.

Writing about suppositions is different from using them to guide research. You should think of suppositions as expository devices by which to point readers to the heart of a problem investigated. As expository or rhetorical devices in a thesis, suppositions are usually better developed than they were in the early stages of investigation.

Some research strategists have objected to the use of suppositions as guides for doing research. (The word *hypothesis* has the same negative effect for them.) These interpreters have argued that suppositions represent biases that restrict an investigator's search and limit his or her understanding of phenomena. Suppositions expressed after the completion of research, however, do not have these disadvantages. In written exposition, a supposition is a means of interpretation that expresses only what the investigator believes after the investigation is complete.

Formality of a Supposition (a Hypothesis)

The language of suppositions can be more or less formal. Formal expression is best, for it explicitly identifies a supposition. One way to do this is to separate the expression physically from the rest of the text (i.e., leave space above and below the statement). Another way is to precede the statement with either the word *supposition* or the word *hypothesis;* do at least this much (e.g., "Supposition 1: Whenever A appears, B is present"). An illustration of formal expression follows:

My supposition was: Small children demonstrate a concept of cardinal number by counting before they demonstrate it in a one-to-one correspondence task.

Placement of a supposition with an explanatory or operational expression shows the level of its generality. A supposition can be stated within an explanatory or an operational expression of a problem, or both. Suppositions given with an explanatory expression fit many phenomena. Looking back at Figure 3.1, you see a supposition expressed abstractly at level 2; it has wide application, or is important because of its generality. In deciding how generally to express a supposition in your own work, be guided by what effect the level of generality will have on your readers' understanding of the problem.

Research strategists cannot satisfy an abstract or general supposition by carrying out some single investigation. When the research evidence is gathered, it will be limited to a small part of what a general supposition covers. If suppositions were to be stated at both level 2 and level 1, the evidence would respond best to the level 1 supposition.

In most graduate student research, suppositions are stated specifically (operationally at level 1, Figure 3.1). These specific suppositions respond more convincingly to the evidences of data than do suppositions at higher levels of abstraction.

Empirical questions are not suppositions.   Empirical questions are casual, relatively uncomplicated questions and therefore are not suppositions. In particular, they show no commitment to a proposition; that is, they are expressions of ignorance and are completely neutral to a set of conditions. Immanuel Kant (1965, p. 93) said: "thoughts without content are empty," and "intuitions without concepts are blind." So also are empirical questions.

Some research needs no supposition because it is not problematic in the ordinary sense.   There are kinds of investigations where suppositions are not needed. A bureau survey of economic conditions or of attitudes may be such a case. No supposition applies if you are not attempting to generate explanations for phenomena, as may be true where data is gathered to form data banks. The weather service, for example, keeps records over long periods of time; such data gathering is not primarily for the purpose of searching for weather explanations, although at a later time the data may be used to explain. Similarly, economic surveys are often made periodically to keep tabs on certain indicators, not to make economic theory.

No supposition is needed for a list of independent questions of roughly equal importance. That also holds for a list of attitude scales or scales of other psychological or social phenomena, unless there is some organized concept linking the scales together to form a common supposition.

Investigations without suppositions, those that describe only what happens to appear, are not conceptual enough to make good topics for graduate research. What would a student put in a proposal? Proposals anticipate a structure that is meaningful; the need for suppositions has nothing to do with kind or method of research.

How to Express Suppositions

State suppositions in present tense, not as predictions.   For example:

Correct:	Children acquire a concept of up–down before a concept of left–right.
Incorrect:	Children *will* acquire a concept of up–down before a concept of left–right.

State suppositions as positive assertions, not empirical questions.   For example:

Correct:	Children acquire a concept of up–down before a concept of left–right.
Incorrect:	Do children acquire concepts of up–down and left–right at the same time?

Present tense shows that the range of application is general. Suppositions always refer to an entire class of phenomena that the research addresses; they are not about a particular instance or a particular research prediction. A researcher wants to know whether to affirm a supposition on the basis of evidence from a carefully constructed sample (an inference, usually statistical). Inferences refer to general positive assertions, not to specific outcomes or forecasts.

State suppositions in their substantive form.   Both the correct and incorrect suppositions in the preceding example are in substantive form. That is, the statements are assertions or expressions of an investigator's beliefs about some particular issue.

Never state null hypotheses in your research report, thesis, or dissertation.   It is not useful to express null hypotheses as representing your research suppositions. Such representations, as convolutions of your substantive alternative suppositions, are confusing for your readers. Because null hypotheses are intrinsic to the logic of inferential statistics, their written expression is superfluous. People who understand inferential logic will always assume that null hypotheses are being tested. If this point is unclear to you, ask a statistical logician for a thorough explanation.

Suppositions (hypotheses) are expressed:

1. At an abstract or *explanatory* level of discourse (at level 2, Figure 3.1). For these expressions, however, the data analysis will offer only indirect support because the actual research operations are at some conceptual distance from the supposition.

2. At a concrete or *operational* level of discourse (at level 1, Figure 3.1). Suppositions composed of concrete language usually are supported directly by the data analysis.

3. At *both* explanatory and operational levels of discourse. The practice of expressing a supposition at two levels shows an investigator's interest in the general supposition (level 2) but acknowledges an indirect attack on that problem by a more specific supposition (level 1). The problems at the two levels, though related, are not the same.

4. Formally. Formal expressions can be separately identified from other parts of a problem statement and are preceded by the word *supposition* or *hypothesis*.

5. In multiples. There are two ways to give multiple suppositions. The first is serially within paragraphs, like this: I tested three hypotheses as follows:
    (a) Children acquire a concept _____, etc. (b) Children learn the meaning _____, etc. (c) Children after the age of six are able to _____, etc.
    The second is serially between paragraphs, like these three paragraph openings: I tested three hypotheses, as follows:
    H_1: Children acquire a concept _____, etc.
    H_2: Children learn the meaning _____, etc.
    H_3: Children, after the age of six, are able to _____, etc.

7. As positive general assertions in present tense, but never as specific predictions in future tense.

8. In their original substantive form, but never as null hypotheses.

Suppositions should be few in number and central to the research problem.

Limit the number of suppositions in a research report. Base your study on one, two, or three suppositions, not more. You trivialize your research if you break down a problem to a long list of minor suppositions. Too many suppositions are as bad as none; at either extreme, you give the impression that there was no research problem to investigate. Write only suppositions that are central to the problem; a single supposition may be enough. Good research is unified under one or two main hypothetical concepts.

A hunch is a supposition. The word *hunch* may sound too casual for research, but some suppositions are little more than hunches. If 10 people have hunches (suppositions) to explain something, there will be 10 different sets of arguments for the hunches. These arguments, called presuppositions, range from hazy and uncritical to precise and logical. The important point here is that the quality of the arguments or presuppositions varies widely, and the success of research depends on how well a report argues its case. A collection of presuppositions may be so forceful as to make an untried supposition thoroughly compelling, or the presuppositions may weakly aggregate to the support of a supposition.

PRESUPPOSITIONS

Recall that presuppositions are a set of propositions that, taken together, lead one to a supposition. Presuppositions are part of the process of discovery; having identified and thought about them, you may come to realize that a set of presuppositions logically evokes a supposition. Then, an explanatory expression of a research problem consists of one or more suppositions, each supported by its own set of presuppositions.

A presupposition is a truth, a postulate, or a principle, but never the same truth or postulate as a supposition itself. The relation of presuppositions to a supposition is that of preceding events leading logically to a conclusion. To examine the relation inversely, a supposition depends on presuppositions for its justification. If supposition A depends on X, Y, Z, then these are three presuppositions of A. As presuppositions, X, Y, and Z may act together or independently in arguing the case of A.

Presuppositions should be expressed in a rhetorical style capable of showing the strength of the supposition they support. What you write in a research report leads readers to ask, "How has the credibility of this supposition changed during the course of the present investigation?" All of the presuppositions, together with the results of data analyses, will determine how believable the supposition is. To examine relations between presuppositions and a supposition, consider the following supposition:

> All objects released from the same point in space and falling freely in a vacuum accelerate at the same rate, regardless of their densities, and reach the same position in space at the same velocity.

The supposition is without basis *unless* we can list arguments for it; we therefore offer these presuppositions:

Presupposition 1: Mass is not the basis for acceleration, nor is it the basis for instantaneous velocity of falling objects. A writer will follow with empirical and analytical evidence, for example the experiments of Galileo showing that mass does not affect acceleration or velocity.

Presupposition 2: Acceleration is due solely to gravity, and gravity is constant for all bodies. Next appears the evidence for presupposition 2.

Presupposition 3: Acceleration of falling objects will depend on the medium through which the object falls. In a complete vacuum, acceleration of all objects will be the same. An explanation follows of the relative impedance to falling objects of various media through which objects might fall. Archimedes' equation relating two densities, density of a falling object and density of a medium, to *apparent weight* is one form of argument for presupposition 3.

No Presuppositions, No Basis

If a supposition lacks presuppositions to back it up, then there is no basis for the assertion. When there are no presuppositions, writers tend to discuss issues generally related to their expressed supposition without setting out the reasons that their suppositions should be believed. This gives readers the impression that the writer simply investigated a number of ideas in a vague, general way, and reported whatever happened to occur. Experienced researchers are analytical; they usually have reasons for their suppositions. Although good presuppositions are not easily derived, they usually can be provided when investigators take the time to investigate and think logically about a problem.

Realistically, much research in the social sciences has a less satisfactory basis in presuppositions than is true in the so-called hard sciences. Although you should always prefer a firm, complete presuppositional basis, you cannot write beyond the realities. Your presuppositions cannot be any better than your reason and judgment permit. Take account of the credibility of each presupposition you write. If you do a lot of thinking when you write a thesis proposal, forming presuppositions that seem possible at that time and continue to rethink the basis as your research continues, then it will not be so difficult to prepare the final document when the time comes. As the investigation proceeds, you will need good notes from your reading and thinking.

Origins of Presuppositions

Presuppositions have almost limitless origins, as Kaplan (1964) noted: "from other sciences, from everyday knowledge, from the experiences of conflict and frustration which motivated our inquiry, from habit and tradition, from who knows where" (p. 87). You may either find or invent propositions to serve as presuppositions from (a) the research findings or theories of others; (b) from your own data, obtained now or long ago; or (c) even from your incidental and informal observations. The origin is less important than how well they fit with other presuppositions and, ultimately, how convincing they are as the basis for a supposition.

Not all the empirical sources of presuppositions are in published literature. Successful investigators have often made use of common observations. Torricelli (1608–1647), for example, noticed that ordinary water pumps seem limited to pumping water only to a certain height, perhaps 32 feet at sea level (a proposition). From his observation, he formed a supposition that a sea of air presses on the surface of the earth, creating pressure such that water from a pump could be raised only so high. At the instant Torricelli formed the supposition about a sea of air, the proposition about pumping limits became a presupposition. The limits of a pump were not presuppositional until Torricelli made the association to his theoretical idea of a sea of air pressing down and recognized that the water could be raised only to a limit imposed by the air pressure.

As research proceeds, when are presuppositions conceived? Usually, propositions (concepts one can believe) are recognized one at a time in the early or preinvestigation period. These propositions are not yet presuppositions. When you begin your research, you must identify and assemble concepts and propositions in an effort to give order to them. Not until a supposition is evolved do some of the propositions become presuppositions. The label *presupposition* is applied only when a proposition becomes an argument for a supposition.

What is called a supposition will always be called a supposition, and all propositions that support the supposition will always be called presuppositions. Nevertheless, what was once a supposition may later also be a presupposition for a new supposition, while still remaining a supposition in its own right.

Before testing a supposition in formal research, you need to have a minimum number of presuppositions that give you sufficient reason to go forward with the research. As research proceeds and you rethink the problem, you will likely derive new presuppositions and discard or revise unsatisfactory ones. Reports of research are argumentative activities, meant to convince an investigator first and others later on. All the arguments will not occur at once, but when you write, all presuppositions for a particular supposition should be argued.

About presuppositions:

1. Presuppositions are the justifications for suppositions.
2. If there are multiple suppositions, each supposition has its own set of presuppositions. Ordinarily, a presupposition does not apply to more than one supposition.
3. A collection of presuppositions attached to their supposition is a complete rationale, which constitutes the major part of an introduction. The only other element is an operational expression of a problem.
4. Presuppositions vary in the quality of their arguments. Some give a good basis for a supposition; others give a less satisfactory basis.
5. A presupposition is never the same concept as the supposition it supports.

Presuppositions originate from propositions found in:

1. Others' research
2. Others' theories
3. Your own research, recent or long past
4. Your incidental and informal observations
5. Your thinking and symbolic interpretations

Thinking is an important source of presuppositions.   Some arguments for suppositions may have no direct ties to observations but may derive entirely from thinking. An illustration of thinking as a source of presuppositions is Albert Einstein's thought experiments, experiments composed entirely of imaginary operations (for example, sending hypothetical elevators to the moon and thinking about what velocity is theoretically possible). Some of the suppositions of relativity theory were derived and tested mentally by creating presuppositions entirely in the imagination.

Einstein, more than many others, emphasized the analytical aspect of science. When others referred to his work as nonempirical, however, he did not agree, because he interpreted the mental events as having sufficient empirical ties.

Counterpresuppositions: Unfavorable Arguments

Seldom do all the evidences agree with a supposition. Successful investigators have learned how to take into account contrary evidence and also recognize the need to report it. We have called favorable arguments *presuppositions;* unfavorable arguments can thus be called *counterpresuppositions.*

Laudan (1977, p. 31) has described the work of Prout, a chemist who in 1815 advanced a supposition that all elements are composed of hydrogen, a general assertion that cannot be tested by a single experiment. Prout then presented his arguments (presuppositions) favoring this supposition.

A *general supposition:* All elements are composed of hydrogen (belongs at level 2, Figure 3.1).

Prout then reduced his general supposition to an operational one, a supposition that can be put to experimental test.

An *operational supposition:* If all elements are composed of hydrogen, then all elements have atomic weights that are integral multiples of the atomic weight of hydrogen (belongs at level 1, Figure 3.1).

In 1815, however, there was current knowledge that was contrary to Prout's operational supposition. We will call this contrary information *counterpresuppositional.*

Counterpresupposition believed in 1815: Some elements have atomic weights that are not integral multiples of the atomic weight of hydrogen; for example, chlorine, 35.45; barium, 68.7; lead, 103.5 (the modern figures are quite different for barium, [137.34] and for lead [207.19]).

When there are positive evidences (presuppositions) to favor a supposition (or a theory), one may have enough confidence to argue for that supposition, as Prout did. He nevertheless had to acknowledge contrary evidence (the counterpresupposition). Explanatory expressions of research problems not only argue the positive evidence but also acknowledge contrary arguments and, when possible, explain these contrary evidences. It is not unusual, however, for one who offers a supposition to have no satisfactory explanation for counterpresuppositional information. Laudan (1977) has called these aberrations in theory *anomalies*. Anomalies are common, even to suppositions that have good standing in science. Belief in a supposition, despite its anomalous character, depends on how many of the relevant phenomena are satisfied by the supposition.

Sometimes anomalies are solved, improving the credibility of a supposition. Long after Prout's time, in the twentieth century, a concept of isotopes was invented. Physical chemists were then able to separate homogeneous isotopes, which have in each case atomic weights that are, in fact, integral multiples of the weight of hydrogen. This new knowledge resolved the counterpresupposition. Had such knowledge been available to Prout, he would have expressed a presupposition about isotopes, which would have removed all the exceptions to his supposition.

Research to Oppose a Supposition

Sometimes research is done to discredit a widely believed supposition. In such a case, one must be able to respond to the presuppositions that support that supposition. Take the case of a general belief that social learning is based largely on the imitation of social behaviors one observes in others. Edward L. Thorndike (1913) once argued that imitation of behavior is not an important basis for learning (his countersupposition). However, he had to account for those cases of imitation we all see. He acknowledged that humans smile when smiled at but interpreted such smiles as mechanical—not associated with a general class of behaviors (his presupposition).

As part of his argument, Thorndike also acknowledged that a collection of birds on a telegraph wire will, when one bird leaves, tend to fly away together. This, too, he interpreted as a minor behavior mechanism but not as a signal that birds learn from imitating each other. Both common observations, of people smiling and birds flying, are evidence (a presupposition), that imitation occurs. Thorndike attempted to limit that presupposition as having only a narrow application.

Reporting Replications

A special kind of literature that we have not discussed up to now is replications. Replications are of two kinds; we must decide what to do with each and whether presuppositions can be derived from them.

Simple replications. Simple replications are repetitions in detail of a previous study, in order to see if repeating the study will reproduce the result of the first attempt. A simple replication tests the *same* supposition as the one previously tested, and all of the earlier presuppositions are still potential arguments that can be used in the replication. Simple replications are unlikely candidates for graduate studies because the one who replicates contributes nothing to the idea content.

Suppose you are an investigator who is doing a simple replication of a ten-year-old study by Jones. Jones's supposition then was exactly the same supposition you hold now. Moreover, since your study will be the same as that of Jones, you have inherited all of Jones's arguments (presuppositions) if you want them. When you cite Jones's study, as you must, however, you are *not* thereby creating a presupposition. Whether or not your results are the same as those of Jones, the citation does not create a presupposition for your study. All a simple replication represents is evidence that an earlier result is probably reliable.

Systematic replications. Systematic replications are partial repetitions of an original study, but with deliberate variations (see Sidman, 1960). These non-duplicating variations of an original are usually conducted to test the range of a supposition—how general it is. The investigator can test points along an independent variable that are different from the original ones to see if these different scale values have the same relative effects on a dependent variable as the original points did. With such variations, an investigator may have a different supposition than was found in the study being systematically replicated.

If you do a systematic replication of an earlier study, then you must decide which, if any, of the earlier investigator's arguments are congruent with your own supposition. If some of them are, use them to support your supposition. Some of the earlier investigator's presuppositions may logically function as counterpresuppositions (against your supposition). If so, simply acknowledge those unfavorable arguments. As with simple replications, the mere citation of the study you are systematically replicating does not constitute an argument (a presupposition). *You must express the presuppositional concept from the study that gives logical grounds for the supposition you have advanced.*

Writing about Presuppositions

Reveal a supposition before its presuppositions. Your ideas will have a better flow and your readers will understand them more easily if you express a supposition before listing the presuppositions on which it is based. You can decide the best order for revealing your presuppositions. If there are many presuppositions, it is best to give them in direct order of their quality as arguments supporting your supposition. Refer back to the Harlow example and think about what constitutes a good order for a reader to follow.

Use labels for presuppositions. Although you do not have to label your arguments *presuppositions,* the advantage of a label is that it requires you, the writer, to identify the words making up the argumentative expression. The label shows that you know that you are giving a basis for a supposition. Some people call such rhetoric a *rationale.*

For example, in the supposition that acceleration is the same for all objects falling through a vacuum, there are three presuppositions, labeled and numbered for identification. Numbering may also help readers to see the succession of arguments. *Paragraphs or even pages that explain each presupposition should follow each of them in turn.*

Show the closeness of a relation between presuppositions and the supposition they support. In the Harlow example, there are two presuppositions. One of these, the presupposition claiming that innate sex differences prepare a mother for motherhood, lies at some conceptual distance from the supposition it supports: that contact comfort is a relatively strong agent in forming a bond from infant to mother. The support is *inferential.* A reader will make inferences from what is written (the presupposition) to the supposition. Sometimes the relation must pass through a chain of presuppositions, where one presupposition supports another presupposition, which in turn supports another, until a basis is built for a supposition. If a reader fails to form the linkages intended to join presupposition to supposition, then the writer has failed. Most of us will not be explicit enough, but it is not easy to discover our failure. One can ask a friend but naive readers are apt to mislead us either because they want to offer a favorable response or because they simply do not understand that they do not understand.

Identify the major presuppositions explicitly. Notice that although only two presuppositions are stated explicitly in the Harlow example, as you read the text there are a larger number of propositions that could justifiably be called presuppositions (for example, "Girls respond to all babies"). As was done in the example, it is best to identify only major presuppositions and subordinate the minor ones under them. Your written exposition will become too complex if you label minor arguments as presuppositions.

Presuppositions Are a Literature Review and More

Unfortunately, research reports seldom identify the presuppositions that are bases for suppositions. Sometimes a reader may be able to extract presuppositions from text that implies them, or create them from propositions that are in the text. Journal editors and other experienced readers see many manuscripts in which a research problem was not well developed because the concepts were not given a good grounding or based on a set of coherent arguments. To avoid this pitfall, you need presuppositions that are well organized and interrelated by the language used. Then, your presuppositions will add up to such a set of coherent arguments.

Merely citing references does not provide a basis for a problem. The Council of Biology Editors' *Style Manual,* fourth edition (1978), says that citations should be "unmistakably relevant to" a problem reported (p. 10). Similarly, the *Publication Manual of the American Psychological Association,* third edition (1983), says that you should "cite only that research pertinent to the specific issue and avoid references with only a tangential or general significance. If you summarize earlier works, avoid nonessential details" (p. 25).

It is not enough for references to be related in some way to a research problem; many kinds of relationships are possible, some of them quite remote. Choose a heading that will remind you as writer to make your citations cohere as a set of historical or logical events.

Headings including the word "Presuppositions" or the phrase "History of the Problem" are good because they call for the use of citations that are relevant to a supposition. Think of such an aggregation as a rationale for the invention of a research problem or, more particularly, for the invention of a supposition.

Write headings that effectively stimulate readers' anticipation. "History of the Problem" and "Presuppositions Leading to the Problem" are headings that are likely to succeed in leading readers forward.

AN OPERATIONAL EXPRESSION OF A PROBLEM

An operational expression of a research problem is the problem reduced to research operations. Of the many studies that could be developed from an explanatory expression (level 2, Figure 3.1), this is only one. Further, this particular study or operational problem is the investigator's choice because it best represents that investigator's *strategy*. Why do you need an operational expression of your problem? An operational statement provides closure for readers. It identifies precisely what the problem was among the various explanatory concepts.

What happens when writers omit operational problem statements? Then, readers must keep in mind the explanatory problem laid out in the introductory paragraphs and construct their own problem reduction (operational problem) while reading procedures in a method section. That's a difficult task.

The language of operations is transactional; it says *what was done*. A complete problem statement in a research report includes both an explanatory expression and an operational expression because they have complementary meanings. An introduction to a thesis is concluded with an operational expression of a problem and followed by a method section delineating the details of the method.

The operational expression should follow the explanatory expression immediately, so that readers can see where the problem fits among the general phenomena (where it lies within the empirical scope of that explanatory problem statement). Readers can then understand, before reading a detailed method section, what possible inferences might be drawn from the study.

Explanatory expressions of problems are lexical definitions, highly dependent on the various meanings attached to words. In contrast, operational expressions depend more on the concrete images they evoke for readers. *These images are big-picture images; they do not include details of method.*

How to Begin an Operational Problem Statement

In order to provoke big-picture images, an operational statement should begin with words like, "In order to show that [such and such] is greater than [such and such], I did this _____. Or: "To demonstrate the [such and such] reaction, I chose to put A at the point in variable X where it should give its most pronounced effect, namely at point [such and such]." The concept will be clear to you when you understand that your words should focus on the strategy, not on details.

Operations as Research Strategy

When an investigator invents research operations to conduct research, these operations are likely to be somewhat removed from an original problem; that is, the operations necessarily create a more restricted problem than was contained in the abstract explanatory expression. You cannot invent operations that fit all the ramifications of an explanatory expression, but you can choose those select operations that you believe will best argue the relevant supposition.

Choosing Transactions to Write About

Operational expressions of research problems are easy to write provided you see their purpose: *to point readers to that limited and special place among variables where an investigator has decided to attack a problem.* You need to express the correct physical actions from the research to reveal your strategy.

Operational expressions of problems differ from method and procedure sections. When writing operational expressions of problems, focus only on what is problematic, and write concretely to represent the problem. Details are unnecessary and only cloud the purpose. In a problem statement, do not say, "I asked 40 girls and 40 boys to _____." Say "children" without giving numbers, sexes, or ages, unless one of these factors is truly central to the problem. You are not writing an abstract of a method section; you are exposing the purpose of the study. A method section shows how you controlled extraneous influences. Your method includes the details a reader must study to judge the validity of your research results. The problem statement, however, is not involved in that validity judgment.

The operational expression given in Figure 3.1 is a selection of words to reveal research strategy (the words are not Harlow's; they were written here to illustrate operational expressions):

This experiment was done to test my supposition that a soft mother surface is more important than food for the power of these variables to attract an infant monkey to an artificial mother. To show the power of that soft surface, I constructed from wire two artificial monkeys, and attached wooden heads having eyes, ears, and mouth. To one mother, a soft terrycloth surface was applied; the other was left uncovered. Both mothers were constructed with a body cavity through which a nursing bottle projected.

These artificial mothers were placed side by side at the end of a room, where infant monkeys were introduced to them. Here these babies were observed for behaviors identified as emotional attachment to one or the other surrogate mother—for example, running to her when frightened (dependent variable). The mothers offered four possibilities: a nursing bottle of milk, a mother surface of cloth providing soft contact for infant clinging, both, or neither (independent variable).

Consider what this operational expression has accomplished. It has shown a reader how the abstract problem was attacked. The explanatory problem contains a supposition: Contact comfort with a mother competes well against food for infant attachment to that mother. But that supposition, like any other, requires operations of some kind to demonstrate it. A reader knowing those operations can see the investigator's plan of attack. *Make certain that operational problem statements identify all the important variables studied.*

Operational Expressions in Descriptive Research

In all strategies and methods of research, an operational expression of a problem exposes to readers the intentions of an investigator. In descriptive research the form of the physical transactions is different from those in an experiment, but the difference does not change the value for readers. Here is a fictitious example of an operational expression in a correlation study of personality characteristics:

> To demonstrate children's emotional distress in response to frequency and intensity of exposure to violence, I gave them the Smith (1986) Scale of Childhood Anxiety and my own (Jones, 1991) Inventory of Emotional Responses (with factor X removed). Three indexes of anxiety were then regressed on variables representing exposure to aggression and a child's passive tendencies. . . .
>
> My supposition was that the distress children manifest is proportional to both the frequency and the intensity of their experience with violence measured in the Smith and Jones scales.

In descriptive research, the flow of language is sometimes better when an operational expression is integrated with an explanatory expression. In the hypothetical survey study of management efficiency discussed earlier in this chapter, there is already sufficient operational language integrated with the explanatory language to make a full problem statement.

Operational expressions of research problems are:

1. Brief, often only 3 to 5 sentences. Explanatory expressions are several times that length.
2. Best given in a separate paragraph with a heading like "The Strategy Used in This Study."
3. Given immediately after an explanatory expression.
4. Transactional. They say what was done. Examples:
    (a) An examiner opened the door for some children, but not for others.
    (b) I presented a list of questions to college students, asking them to _____.
    (c) Five-year-olds came one at a time to a room where they chose between _____.
    (d) I first regressed variable Y on the four variables of A–D. Next, . . .
5. Highly select transactions capable of revealing a problem or showing its reduction from an abstract expression.
6. Free of irrelevant details. For example, operational problem statements do not refer to classification variables like age or sex of subjects unless these variables are central to the problem.
7. Complementary in meaning to explanatory expressions. They show what ramification of an explanatory problem was actually examined by research.
8. Expressions of the ways variables were treated in research. All important variables must be identified.

CHAPTER 4

How to Write A Method Section

The method section, which follows immediately after your introduction, allows readers to understand the objectives of your study and judge whether the methods you used can meet those objectives. Satisfactory methods lead to valid generalizations, given in a results section. Your methods themselves should be based on good research strategy, with help from your graduate committee.

Methods are, of course, created as you plan your research and modified as the research proceeds. But the proposed methods may undergo revision as you gather data. Only the final form of these methods should be described in the method section of a thesis.

The title of the section or chapter should be "method" or "methods," never "methodology." *Method* refers to the particular method involved. *Methodology* refers to the general study of methods and involves arguments about what kinds of methods are appropriate.

STYLE, GRAMMAR, AND CONTENT OF METHOD

If your study has been well planned, the method section is the easiest part of a research report to write. Write the method section in a discursive style to avoid the monotony that is common in discussing method. For the most forceful writing, use the first person. Do not hesitate to write, "I brought 10 children to a room, where . . ." If you do hesitate, you can depersonalize the actor by writing, "The investigator brought 10 children . . ."

Much of the method section should be written in past tense ("The examinees *wrote* for 10 minutes"). Some referents are timeless, however, and require present tense ("The apparatus *is* 30 centimeters tall").

The most serious error in the method section is omission of vital information that readers need in order to see the logic of a study and judge the adequacy

---

1. "Method," or "Method and Procedure" in some journals, is a proper heading—never "Methodology."

2. Method is a listing of the tactics of research. It is one of the bases readers have for judging the validity of a study. In the social sciences, those evidences usually include: (a) subjects and design; (b) procedure; (c) materials, measurements, and apparatus used; (d) evidence that statistical and other assumptions have been met; and (e) evidence for validity and reliability of measurements. In other sciences, the list of tactics may be quite different. For example, in chemistry, the list might include: (a) preparation of glassware, (b) preparation of standards, and so on.

3. Place all elements of method (tests of assumptions, reliability, and validity coefficients) here, not in the results section.

4. Use past tense for all past events.

5. Use active voice: "I examined," or "The observer examined."

6. Make a list of elements to cover. Completeness of method is important.

of a method. Reviewers are usually quick to pick up these omissions and sometimes give them disproportionate weight in judging your research, depending on the importance of what is omitted.

Everything that has to do with the validity of the study—design, form of analysis, and instrumentation—belongs in the method section. All tests of statistical assumptions, evidences of test validity and reliability, and threats to the study design belong there. Do not classify elements of your thesis as method or results solely on the basis of whether calculations were involved. Calculations necessary to establish the validity of measurements belong in the method section. The placement of such information under results is a tactical mistake.

The content of the method section, given under conventional subheadings, is treated next in the order in which the elements are usually presented. I have tried to describe the content under each subject in a way that fits a wide range of data-based research in the psychological and social sciences. As you prepare to write your method section, form a list of elements you will cover under each subheading.

SUBJECTS AND DESIGN

With increasing frequency, "Design of the Study" is appearing together with "Subjects" and is usually given first in a method section. The heading is then "Subjects and Design." The combination of these two elements and their placement first under method allow you to give a comprehensive view of the research plan.

A reader should understand early what that research plan is. In particular, multifactored statistical designs and complex nonstatistical designs need exposition under "Subjects and Design." You can see that an operational expression of a problem, placed in an introduction preceding the method section, leads logically to "Subjects and Design." Together, the operational problem statement and the description of subjects and design form a concrete picture of the investigator's purpose. They fill out the strategy and details behind an abstract explanatory expression of a problem.

In studies having a simple design and few factors, readers can anticipate completely how the data will be partitioned. In such simple studies, you should omit design from the heading. For example, after reading an introduction, readers should adequately anticipate a simple two-factor study having no separation of the variables into levels. In that case, you can say under "Subjects" that the subjects were divided into the two factors or that the two factors were given to all the subjects (as successive treatments).

Writing about Subjects

In statistical investigations, two main aspects of the subjects interest readers; these two aspects are those that determine the generality of the research results. The first is the number of subjects at each unit of analysis (separate data group). This number establishes the statistical power of a generalization: The larger the number of subjects, the better. In comparisons between subgroups, the number in the smaller group sets a limit on the statistical inferences an investigator can make. The membership of each subgroup should be large enough for the laws of chance to have a balanced effect.

The other main factor is freedom from bias in the way subjects are obtained. Statisticians prefer a simple random sample from a population, but human and animal subjects are almost never drawn randomly from their populations because we seldom have access to entire populations from which to draw samples. This failure makes knowledgeable readers skeptical of the claim that our samples are free of bias. Commonly, investigators substitute for a simple random sample by obtaining subjects in a way that convinces readers that the sample is not biased by a recognizable factor and by reporting subject selection with sensitivity to readers' interest in bias.

The following is a fictitious report of subject selection where the sample is *not* a simple random sample. Study this fictitious instance for the ways in which number of subjects and bias are treated; in particular, consider sex.

> We accepted subjects one at a time, to a total of 240, as they appeared at our clinic from November 1, 1996, to March 31, 1997. Subjects were assigned randomly to one of six comparison groups ($n = 40$) as they came Monday through Friday, 9:00 A.M. to 5:30 P.M. (the hours the clinic was open). After 200 subjects had been assigned randomly, the remaining 40 were assigned by sex so as to balance sex across the six groups. The largest imbalance among the six groups was rectified first. In all, 111 females and 129 males were assigned. Age of subjects ranged from 26 to 47.

The foregoing selection of human subjects is ordinary, but it is not random. The impression is that this fictitious investigator did what seemed possible within practical limits to get a representative sample. As you might suspect, random assignment of subjects to six comparison groups, as was done by the fictitious investigator, does not create randomness of origin for the subjects. Random *assignment,* however, has its own value. At least, after the subjects were obtained, they were subsequently treated randomly. But random *selection* would mean that they were originally selected from an entire population by a method that gives all individuals an equal chance to be in the sample. In most cases, that is impossible.

The statement reveals common practical constraints on how subjects are usually obtained. Investigators generally fall short of an ideal random sample. In the following excerpts, notice how the statement includes information needed to judge the sample for relative freedom from bias: (a) "one at a time . . . as they appeared at our clinic" shows that this was a select sample excluding patients from all other clinics in the entire population of clinics, and therefore not a random sample; (b) "from November 1, 1996, to March 31, 1997" excludes patients who came from April 1 through October 31; (c) "Monday through Friday, 9:00 A.M. to 5:30 P.M." excludes other days and hours.

You observe that there was an effort, whether a good plan or not, to balance sex across six groups and that the sexes were not equal in the total sample. Sex, age, and any other relevant classification variables should be reported as they were in the fictitious example. The investigator mentioned these classification variables because they were variables he thought a reader might question as possibly adding bias to the criterion measures.

In each case, you must judge whether to mention these classifications of age, sex, socioeconomic status, and the like, on the basis of your judgment of the questions you think readers will raise. More often than not, you should include these descriptions in a section describing the subjects.

A last point about subjects: Never hide a threat of biasing conditions from readers by omitting important information. Regardless of what writers report, readers will make their own judgments of the adequacy of methods. Complete information is more likely to lead to favorable judgments.

In reporting about subjects:

1. Give their number and, when reasonable, the numbers in subgroups (for example, 50 subjects in each subgroup).
2. Give all aspects of subject selection that provide evidence of freedom from bias. Keep in mind an idea of a representative sample or a simple random sample. (Review definitions of *random sample* in a statistics text.)
3. Look at several reports in your field of study to determine what is customarily included under "Subjects." For example, in developmental psychology, mean age and standard deviation, sex, race, ethnic group, amount of education, and the like are common. Each of these is a potential source of bias.
4. Place the design of the study under the same heading as the subjects, or place the design in a succeeding paragraph with its own heading.

Writing about Design

Having read in your introduction a research problem expressed as operations or physical transactions, your readers will understand the *general strategy* of your research. In the method section, on reaching the subhead "Design," readers will learn the particulars (details and tactics). Design makes your strategy explicit. Readers benefit from a design section when an investigator tells how a total subject pool has been partitioned into comparison groups, thereby creating a complete description of a plan of attack (or when data are partitioned according to the variables studied). In statistical research, analysis of variance and multivariate analysis often need design exposition. One way to make the dimensions of investigation clear is to report the number of comparisons, as in the following fictitious example:

> This was a two-factored analysis of variance, with sex represented at two levels. Equal numbers of subjects were distributed over the comparisons of four (memory strategies) by two (durations of practice) and two (sexes).

Use words to describe the variables, like *memory strategies* and *sexes,* that will be clear to your readers. Do not create labels for the variables that your readers have never seen before.

Include the form of analysis, statistical or other. In the design statement, tell what kinds of analyses were used. If there are any special problems in these analyses, for example a question of whether an assumption (statistical or other) has been met, this is the place to analyze that threat to the validity of the study. *Never* leave such a matter for the results section. Respond to all threats to the validity of your study in the method section, giving *all* the evidence of validity; include the results of mathematical calculations to show that an assumption is robust enough for your study. If you have apparently violated a logical assumption but believe the assumption can tolerate your data, place that argument and the data evidence here.

When exposing your design, identify for readers those sources that have helped you shape your strategy. Avoid complicated symbolism. But when you do choose to use notation to describe your design, make sure it can be understood, and cite a source for such notation. The numerous sources explaining statistical design include:

> *Experimental Design: Procedures for the Behavioral Sciences* (Kirk, 1982)
>
> *Quasi-experimentation, Design and Analysis Issues for Field Settings* (Cook & Campbell, 1979)
>
> *Statistical Principles in Experimental Design* (Winer, 1979)
>
> *Design and Analysis: A Researcher's Handbook* (Keppel, 1982)
>
> *Exploratory Data Analysis* (Tukey, 1977)

PROCEDURE

A procedure section gives readers the essential tactics that fill out a research strategy. You must decide how much detail to give; you should include only those procedural elements needed to understand what took place. Report the successive aspects of the research so that readers understand the temporal progression of what you did ("I presented *X* and asked subjects to do *Y*. I next gave them . . .").

Where the procedures of a study can be questioned or issues raised about whether the study can reach the objectives you have set for it, you should spell out the procedures fully and accurately without using defensive language. Tell what you did to overcome certain strategic problems.

Frequently, the key aspect of a research problem is represented by printed statements given to subjects. Suppose, for example, that your study was about cognition in adults. In this case, you might choose to quote verbatim from instructions given to subjects, or whatever else would reveal your research strategy for the cognitive issue. In reading through your procedures, readers will be thinking about how well these procedures fit with the rationale for the study, and be looking for indications that the procedures satisfy a particular problem, not some general problem.

Usually it is not necessary to report verbatim instructions to subjects. All studies, however, have their own special problems or intrinsic threats to their validity; therefore, each investigator must understand what procedures need special treatment so that readers can see how that investigator dealt with the threats.

Research is a strategic exercise; the tactics are merely aspects of the strategy. Do not overexplain by giving details that are irrelevant for readers trying to judge how well the research operations fit the strategy. As the writer, you are responsible for choosing what to write in order to give the essence of a plan. Outline the general procedure, but refer to the details only when they represent points of vulnerability in your plan that readers should or will question. Remember, all research has its points of vulnerability.

MATERIALS, APPARATUS, TESTS

Describe the essential materials used in the study. Obviously, unique apparatus or paper-and-pencil materials need fuller description than standard materials. Consider using drawings or photographs of complex apparatus to avoid cumbersome verbal descriptions. Standard equipment can be referenced by manufacturer and model number. If paper-and-pencil instruments are brief, they can be reproduced verbatim (for example, a survey having 10 or fewer short, simple items).

VALIDITY AND RELIABILITY OF MEASUREMENTS

A method section should include arguments for the validity of your measures or observations. Are the observations you made and the data you gathered really what you claim they are? For research to convince your readers, the dependent measurements must be valid. You must tell what it is that shows that each measure you have used really is the concept you claim it is. Suppose, for example, that you are studying the motivation of children to persist at a difficult task. You might have subjects work at such a task and measure the time they continue working. Is time spent at that task a valid measure of persistence? To some degree it is valid; but if the subjects do not show an intense interest in the task, or if they do irrelevant things, then the validity of time at the task as a measure of persistence becomes uncertain.

Validity of measurements is so important that it should have high priority in a method section. A study cannot be valid if the measures used or the observations reported are not themselves valid. Reliability of measures is always secondary to validity because reliability is only one of several arguments for validity. Therefore, place reliability under the validity arguments. If, for example, you have three measures of the same or different concepts, give the evidence separately for each measure and place the evidence of reliability under the evidence of validity. A measure must be reliable to be valid, but a measure is not valid simply because it is reliable. Measures that are reliable are not useful unless they are also valid.

For published tests and inventories, there are several kinds of validity arguments. If you use a standard test or inventory, identify the kind of validity that can be argued for that test and reference your arguments by a citation (classes of validity such as content, predictive, concurrent, and the like).

The term *content validity* applies to an argument that the content of a measure fits its label. It is an argument that the content of some subject matter has been proportionately sampled in each of its major subtopics. If a test has too many items of one kind and too few of another, that test is not valid for the label the test carries. If, for example, we consider a test of algebra knowledge, then the items of the test must cover, in appropriate proportions, the main topics deemed essential to a knowledge of algebra. There should be neither too many nor too few items covering for example, factoring.

Publishers of tests and inventories should provide validity arguments in their manuals, but sometimes they do not. See *Buro's Mental Measurement Year-books* for reviews of tests. Reviewers typically give both sides of a validity argument. If generally acknowledged arguments are lacking, then you should give whatever evidence you can. State briefly what conceptual basis there is for the validity of your measurement.

One form of validity evidence is a correlation coefficient. If two dimensions are meant to represent the same thing and one dimension is already accepted as valid, then a high correlation between the two strengthens the argument that the second is also valid. A correlation index of a relation between measures is helpful, but such a number (or even several correlation indices) cannot establish the validity of that instrument.

Validity is often a relative concept, and therefore a weak one. Sufficient validity is not established merely by any positive evidence, however small its magnitude, or by any statistical index. Rather, validity means that the measure is genuinely satisfactory for the purpose you claim it has. You should argue that the measure really accomplishes what it is supposed to do.

CHAPTER 5

How to Write
a Results Section

If an introduction is the expression of a problem, then a results section is a response to that problem. One follows from the other. The first sentence in a results section gets right to the point, giving the results that respond to a problem. Do not think of results as an assembly of numbers or data, but as arguments for and against the suppositions in a research problem. In the results section, you will want to approach the problem from as many angles, or arguments, as will convince readers of your interpretation of the evidences. Results should always begin with data evidences that respond directly to a research problem; anything else is inappropriate for the results section. In particular, aspects of method and procedure do not belong there.

Results respond to a problem. To test the appropriateness of information for placement in a results section, consider:

1. The directness by which the results respond to a research question. If the question is, "What color is that?," then the answer is a color, not, "This is a latex-based paint." Similarly, a research question is answered by results.
2. Its argumentative value. A results section is composed of evidence for suppositions.

Numbers or words about analyses do not, by themselves, qualify as results.

To write results, you need a correct mental set. Think of the correct content and correct order of presentation. Remember to give the most important evidence first.

PRIMARY OR DESCRIPTIVE EVIDENCE

Whatever strategy of investigation you have followed, a description of what you have observed always comes first in your report. This primacy of description is true whether you have gathered statistical evidence or have some other type of empirical evidence, like the verbal descriptions of tribal groups common to social anthropology. There are no exceptions. These descriptive data are called the *primary evidence* because of their central place in an argument. Your readers will first want a description of your observations as an investigator.

If the description is in the form of numerical averages and variations, then statistical means and standard deviations are the first evidences given in results. These evidences are called *descriptive statistics* because they describe the outcome of investigation in the most essential and primary way.

Two Classes of Evidence in Results Sections of Research Reports

Primary evidence (description) and secondary evidence (inference) are the two forms of evidence given in scientific argument. *Description* is a faithful reporting of what actually occurred (indexes of *sample* observations—that is, means, proportions, standard deviations). *Inference* is a generalization extending from sample observations to an *entire population*.

It should be clear from the following analogy that description must come first. Suppose you have witnessed an automobile accident; a crowd has gathered, and the police have arrived. A policeman will ask you what happened, and you must decide what to say and in what order. You can begin correctly by describing what you saw, *or* you can make the mistake of forming inferences and give these first. It would be wrong to say, "The driver of the blue car was at fault." Always give a description first. Logically, one must know the facts before making inferences. The same is true in research reports; give the descriptive evidence first. *Never begin with inferential statistics,* and do not first give a probability for one of these statistics (such as $t = 2.6$, $p = .007$; or $F = 5.68$, $p = .001$).

Some Kinds of Primary Evidence

Numerical description. Numbers as a sample set of observations are called descriptive statistics. These include the original variates you write down as measurements, the average of the variates, their standard deviation, and the number of variates.

In writing a results section for a research report, you can give descriptive statistics as numerals in text, or they can be organized in a table or shown more abstractly in a figure. More will be said later about these forms of data presentation.

Verbal description. In some research reports, words describing a set of related observations may be the only form of description. These reports may contain few or no numbers. In some fields of study, numbers may not fit the evidence obtained, or an investigator may not think of an effective way to gather numerical evidence. For example, a very complex social context may not easily reduce to a numerical abstraction; a sociologist might therefore attempt to convince a reader by verbally describing certain interrelations among variables. These verbal descriptions are likely to contain varying degrees of subjectivity, depending on what is described and how the description is given. An investigator is free to use verbal, numerical, and statistical evidence all in the same report if all three types of evidence will support an argument.

Verbal description has been common in the field of anthropology. Anthropologists have used the term *ethnographic method* to describe strategies of description and inference that seem especially appropriate to their field of study. Professionals in other fields have recently become interested in ethnographic methods and have begun to use them in studies of nursing, teaching, and other complex, dynamic circumstances.

Regardless of the research strategy, description will always precede inference. In research, *description* means describing what you have observed among the variables being studied.

An Example of Primary Evidence in a Statistical Investigation

The example that follows shows how you might set out descriptive evidence in a results section. Description occurs abruptly at the very beginning of results. The example is based on an imaginary study of adults' memory for words that are

Descriptive evidence, which comes first in a results section, may be given in many forms; among them are:

1. Numerals entered in text
2. Numerals entered in a table
3. Lines or other symbols entered in a figure to represent numerals
4. Narratives, as commonly used in anthropology, archaeology, and sociology

Descriptive evidence, in the form of statistics, includes any numerical evidence that describes only a sample set of observations but not a population from which the observations were drawn. Examples of such statistics are:

1. A mean, a median, or an original observation
2. A standard deviation, a variance, or a range
3. A number, such as number of observations made
4. A proportion, a percentage, or another transformation to describe a characteristic in a sample
5. A correlation coefficient, but *not* its probability (that is, no *p*-values, such as $p = .03$).

related with varying degrees of closeness to a stimulus word. Before the example is an illustration of how memory might suffer by the distance in meaning separating as associated word from a stimulus word. In other words, the closer the relation of a stimulus word (*horse*), to a response word (such as *saddle*), the better a person's memory will be.

	ASSOCIATIVE DISTANCE OF A WORD RELATION			
STIMULUS	1	2	3	4
Horse	Saddle	Hay	Cowboy	Crime

In response to a stimulus word *horse, saddle* was assumed to be the most recallable word and *crime* the least recallable.

Results

My subjects' memories were close to what I had expected. Memory was best for words closely associated in meaning with a stimulus word. Table 5.1 shows the mean numbers of words remembered, standard deviations, and proportions of words remembered. Notice that the difference in memory that separates remoteness of word relations 2 and 3 is not as great as between the other two steps of relatedness. I take that inequality of separation in the empirical data to reflect imperfect intervals of association linking stimulus word to associated words.

TABLE 5.1   Number of Words Recognized and Recalled According to a Word's Associative Distance from a Stimulus Word

	ASSOCIATIVE DISTANCE OF A WORD RELATION			
KIND OF MEMORY	1	2	3	4
Recognition:				
Mean numbers	114.00	94.00	83.00	35.00
Standard deviations	8.61	7.99	7.75	6.07
Proportions	.95	.78	.69	.29
Recall:				
Mean numbers	85.00	59.00	48.00	2.00
Standard deviations	8.27	7.19	6.36	.08
Proportions	.71	.49	.40	.02

Notice certain things in the illustration.   There is a centered heading, "Results." It is ordinary to use the single word "Results" as a main heading for a section giving evidences. In some journals, the heading "Results and Discussion" is preferred.

The first sentence interprets for readers: "My subjects' memories were close to what I had expected." It is a good idea to give readers a factually based interpretation. On reading the sentence, readers then know immediately how the investigator interpreted the descriptive evidence, namely, "Memory was best for words closely associated in meaning with a stimulus word." There is no inference in that statement; it simply states a fact—what actually occurred in a sample of subjects.

There is a writing principle involved in making interpretations: Write sentences that will help readers find their way to understanding the data. Call attention to certain numbers in the evidences, both those that agree with your supposi-

---

Interpret your presentation for readers:

1. Use words that interpret descriptive statistics as agreeing or disagreeing with your supposition.
2. When your evidences are intrinsically complicated, say what is necessary to help a reader understand what is in a figure or table.
3. Direct a reader's attention to a location in a table if such a location reveals the essence of a result.
4. Create proportions as a means of explicitly showing relative magnitudes.
5. Point to particularly favorable or unfavorable evidence if you think a reader is likely to miss it.

In any of the above, use words that limit your interpretation to description of a sample. Avoid generalizations.

tions and those that disagree. But direct readers only to those evidences that will help them quickly grasp what has occurred. Be a skilled expositor who knows how to present information in a way that will expedite readers' understanding of the data evidences. Research reporters must have no interest in biasing a reader's interpretation, only in helping to make the evidences clear. Interpretations should be held close to the evidence.

Notice that the second sentence in the example refers to Table 5.1. Table 5.1 consists of descriptive data, what is called the primary evidence. The magnitudes of these numbers reveal whether the sample of human subjects manifested memories that agree with the investigator's supposition. In this case, they do agree.

Means, standard deviations, and proportions are the descriptors in the example. Proportions are excellent descriptors, which have been neglected too often by research reporters. *Proportions recognized* is an evidence that complements the mean value (for example, at the first word position, .95 complements 114, the mean). Consider whether proportions will be an appropriate evidence in your own work.

Results should be just long enough to make evidence clear. If there is only one set of descriptive evidences, as in the foregoing example, then all that remains to be written are the inferential evidences. In many cases, however, there are separate arguments represented by separate sets of descriptors (descriptive statistics); each set of descriptors is followed by its own inferential argument (inferential statistics). This is the pattern for reporting results: description, followed by related inferences, followed by other description and related inferences.

Never repeat the evidence. If your results are relatively uncomplicated and take up little space, do not be concerned that your work will look unimportant. In results, short statements that are to the point are preferred. Never allow your discomfort with a short presentation lead you to repeat any of your results or interpretations. Students sometimes make the mistake of repeating themselves, either because they think their ideas will be missed or because they are concerned that their presentation is too brief.

The principle here extends to the form in which you give your data. Never place the same evidence in more than one of the following forms of presentation: (a) text, (b) a table, or (c) a figure. You must choose *one and only one* of these forms and not duplicate the evidence. Resist the temptation to think that your readers will gain different impressions from data in a table and the same data in the form of a figure. You may *interpret* in text what you have presented in a table or figure, but never convey the same information twice. See the discussions on this point in the *Publication Manual of the American Psychological Association* (1983, pp. 27, 80, 83–84).

SECONDARY OR INFERENTIAL EVIDENCE

Once your readers have seen the primary (descriptive) evidences, they will be ready to examine secondary evidences based on them (inferential statistics or other inferential arguments). These secondary evidences are special ways of analyzing the descriptive data to see if a supposition can be argued as probably true of a population.

No inference or generalization can be made from descriptive evidence until that evidence has been given.   Inferential statistics must *always* follow descriptive statistics. All inferential calculations lead to an inferential statistic (such as *t*, *F*, or χ^2) and end in a probability. Such a probability, which is the goal of inferential calculations, is the basis for an inference provided that the probability is small (rare). The purpose of inferential calculations is *always* to arrive at a probability—nothing else. As a statistical argument, only the probability has value for forming an inference (a generalization); all the preliminary work is done simply to arrive at that final probability.

The Rarity Argument

This is an argument that an inference is valid because p *(a probability) is rare.*   Once you have described your sample observations and noted a difference or a relation among variables relevant to your supposition, you will want to form an inference that the difference (or relation) is generally true and not limited to your sample of observations. In statistics, that generalization depends entirely on the size of *p,* which is a proportion of a random distribution of statistics where nothing of substance operates (a proportion of a random variable). A common value like $p = .30$ is not convincing, but a rare value like $p = .0000001$ is.

The inferential argument is this: Suppose an inferential statistic (such as *t* or *F)* that you have calculated is compared to a distribution of random statistics (random *t*s or *F*s) found within a random variable (compared to tabled values of that statistic or compared to random statistics by a computer). Then suppose that within that random variable your inferential statistic is rare or unusual. Why is it rare, if not because your descriptive data are representative or typical of the average of other data that you could obtain if you had the time, patience, and disposition to take all the possible samples like your sample?

You look for a rare *p* because a generalization depends on it. The comparison of an inferential statistic to the values in a random variable is made by a subroutine in a computer that prints out a *p*-value, or it is made by you when you look in a table of random statistics. Random variables generated in a computer are relatively complete, allowing a computer to print a probability (*p*) as equal to a certain proportion. Tables of inferential statistics are skeletal random variables showing only certain selected *p*-values; they are limited by the space available in a table. Because tables do not give exact probabilities, a table allows you to report only that $p <$ a certain proportion; $p = $ a certain proportion almost certainly will not be found in that limited table.

The rarity argument does not lead to a final conclusion. It is, rather, an argument of relative confidence that a generalization is justified. The smaller *p* is, the stronger is your belief that a difference or a correlation is not a random occurrence. For example, an occurrence of one in a million among chance events ($p = .000001$) is more convincing than one in a thousand ($p = .001$), which in turn is more convincing than one in a hundred ($p = .01$). Statistically speaking, confidence in a generalization rests on how rare a result is.

How to Report Probability Evidence

There is good reason to report probabilities to as many decimal places as necessary to give an equality. This means that p will be followed by an equal sign ($=$) rather than a less-than sign ($<$) in order to show how rare your particular inferential statistic is. The practice of showing p to be equal to a certain decimal value is becoming more common because computers can be programmed to calculate the equality and, when you resort to a table (giving $p < .05$, or $p < .01$), you fail to use all of the statistical argument. Not all statistical programs for computers will print the actual probability for your statistic. Look for one that does.

There is a weakening convention to form statistical inferences at just that point where a statistic has been found to have a probability less than $p = .05$. Such an outcome of less than .05 has traditionally been called *statistically significant*. Before the advent of computers, that convention was a convenience to avoid calculating p. All you had to do was look up the inferential statistic in a table and read the corresponding p value at a column head. But tables cannot be large enough to contain the actual statistic you compute, so the practice has been to find the closest smaller table statistic and write p as being less than that statistic (for example: If $t = 2.00$, 70 df, then $p < .05$).

The trouble with this convention of convenience is that it treats confidence as if it worked like a light switch—either *on* ($p < .05$; you believe) or *off* ($p > .05$; you do not believe). In truth, however, human belief or confidence is progressive. The stronger the evidence, the greater our confidence; the smaller p is, the greater is our confidence.

All this discussion of the strength of evidence depends on much more than

---

Secondary evidence is:

1.   Inferential evidence; evidence that a characteristic in a sample is like that characteristic in a population (a generalization: What is true of my observations is also true of the universe from which I took my sample). An inference can be based on an inferential statistic or on *any form of argument that is convincing in the mainstream of science*. Regularities based on observation must be capable of overcoming scientists' skepticism.

2.   Always preceded by descriptive evidence, the primary evidence.

3.   Often gained by calculating an inferential statistic, such as a statistic of t or F, and interpreted according to how unusual that statistic is.

4.   Represented by p, a probability in a random variable (small p means unusual). Only the final probability has a part in the argument.

5.   Best given with p equal to some magnitude. This means that the probability will actually be calculated in a computer and reported to as many decimal places as necessary to give weight to the argument that the statistic is unusual (e.g., $F = 40$, $p = .0006$). The use of the less-than symbol ($p < .05$) eliminates some of that argument.

6.   A weighted argument, and therefore is not directed toward a conclusion but, instead, permits relative confidence.

statistical probability. The quality of your original data, how well they fit or do not fit a scale with mathematical qualities of genuine magnitude, and the quality of your problem and rationale have overriding importance. No statistical analysis, no matter how complex, and no inferential probability, no matter how rare, can make up for deficiencies in the basic problem or in your rationale for its solution.

The Use of Headings to Reveal Inferences

When you have reported all of the descriptive evidence that you intend to report, make relevant inferences you can justify. The first inference to express is in response to the first hypothesis offered in your problem statement. Suppose, for example, you have the following hypothesis: "All objects, regardless of their densities, fall at the same rate in a vacuum." Now suppose also that the inferential analysis you completed agreed with your hypothesis. You may then express in a heading an inference that the hypothesis was supported. That heading might read:

The Evidence Supports My Hypothesis
that All Objects, Regardless
of their Densities, Fall at the Same Rate
in a Vacuum.

Immediately following this heading, an investigator should place the secondary (inferential) evidence. Notice that *the hypothesis has been expressed as a positive, timeless generalization,* as it should be. Hypotheses should *not* be expressed as predictions. Do not write either in future tense ("The objects that I examine in my laboratory *will fall* at the same rate") or in past tense (*"fell"* at the same rate").

The reason is this: The secondary or inferential evidence is evidence about phenomena in the universe or population, not about a sample. Therefore, an unlimited hypothesis (a generalization) fits the logic of inference. The language of prediction misinterprets the purpose of statistical inference, making the hypothesis apply only to a sample of observations rather than to an entire population. Furthermore, the word *hypothesis* conveys the tentativeness of the assertion. Any hypothesis remains tentative and only relatively believable, even after convincing inferential evidence has been presented. *Hypothesis* literally means "thesis standing above" (that is, above the facts and evidences).

Why should an inference be made in a heading? The answer is that your purpose is exposition—making it easy for readers to see quickly what the results were. Also, you are interpreting for readers in a form that is hard to misunderstand.

In the text following an interpretive heading, place whatever evidence is basis for the interpretation given in the heading. A results section organized around headings that give away results is clear and effective. Results can be organized in other ways, but there is no clearer or more expeditious method of presentation.

Now, consider a more complete example that contains an inference expressed in a heading itself, followed by text that gives the evidence supporting it. Assume that the heading and the text following come immediately after the descriptive evidence given in Table 5.1.

An Example of a Heading Containing an Inference Followed by Text Supporting the Inference

A Hypothesis Was Supported that Both Recognition and Recall of a Word Are Proportional to that Word's Associative Proximity to a Stimulus Word.

Repeated-measures analysis of variance was performed on subject's recognition and recall of words in the study. These results were: recognition, $F = 4.83$ (3/10), $p = .025$; recall, $F = 8.08$ (3/10), $p = .005$. Clearly, the evidence agrees with a supposition that memory is best for words closely associated with a stimulus word. To demonstrate proportional memory, I [etc.] . . .

Note: For the sake of simplicity in the illustration, simple analysis of variance was used. In real circumstances, multivariate analysis would have been the method of choice because the dependent variables are correlated.

What to notice in the example. Pay particular attention to the length of the heading. Most headings are shorter than this one. Is it too long? No, it is seldom a mistake to write lengthy headings. Every heading you write should be long enough to be understood. Too often writers compose short, cryptic heads that are not clear. Notice in the heading the conjunction *that* and the preposition *of.* Such prepositions and conjunctions make the expression understandable; without them, you may create an inscrutable noun–adjective string. Notice also that the word order is natural, as it might be in conversation by two investigators. Try to write naturally and without affectation. Avoid words meant to impress and expressions meant to seem complex; such efforts will only have the opposite effect on intelligent readers.

The hypothesis is, as you have learned to expect, written as a generalization. The tense is perennial present tense: "Recognition and recall *are* proportional." The proposition is timeless; it is not something of the past or of the future. Notice, however, that the evidence is bounded by time: "A hypothesis *was* supported."

Not all headings in the results section need to express hypotheses. If there are several lines of attack on a single hypothesis, each of these forms of evidence might appear under a separate heading subordinated to a heading containing a hypothesis. What are called *run-in paragraph headings* are appropriate as subordinated headings. If, in the foregoing example, the evidence were to be divided into two lines of evidence, "Recognition memory" and "Recall memory," then two paragraphs could be formed with these phrases as the paragraph headings just as they appear here. The next heading, beginning "Notice," is a *run-in paragraph heading.*

Notice the inferential interpretation.   It is helpful to readers to know what interpretation you place on your own work. It is not presumptuous to express that inference as long as you limit your interpretation to the evidence. In the example, after giving inferential *F*-statistics, the writer said, "Clearly, the evidence agrees with a supposition that . . ." That sentence is purposeful and justified. The distinction between interpretation and discussion will be made in the next chapter.

If the evidence turned out weak or was completely lacking, you should say so. For example, you might say, "Clearly, the evidence does not support an inference that . . ." The point is not that your readers will miss the statistical evidence; rather, you are being more completely explicit and are making the document more readable. Relatively unsophisticated readers can learn from these interpretive statements how to read and understand research.

Notice that the probability is given as an equality (p =).   The example probabilities have been written with equal signs, as they should be to show the rarity of the *F*-statistics and to allow readers to judge their relative believability. However, some people still prefer to set a standard for rejecting a null hypothesis (for example, $p < .05$) and call such a result *statistically significant*. Determine whether your committee members prefer the actual probability or such a standard, known as an alpha standard.

Some Examples of Headings Where Inferences Are Claimed or Cannot Be Claimed

Your headings should reveal whether or not the evidence was convincing. Readers will understand your document more quickly if your headings include both a supposition and the result of analysis either supporting or not supporting the supposition. When evidence does not develop as you had hoped, you may be inclined to play down the result, but you should not. It is better to make the failure of evidence for an inference as plain as evidence favoring an inference. The following are some examples in which we assume favorable evidence for an inference:

My Supposition Was Supported
that the Rate of Inflation
Is Inversely Related to Interest Rates.

Hypothesis 1 Was Successfully
Demonstrated in Three of Four Tasks,
that Difference in Quickness of Response
Is Due to the Accuracy Demanded
by a Task.

Notice that the words *supposition* and *hypothesis* have been used synonymously. Use either one, but do not use both in the same report.

Now, here are some examples in which we assume evidence is lacking for an inference:

My Hypothesis Was Not Supported,
that Middle-Income Families Take Greater
Investment Risks than High-Income
Families.

A Supposition that Empathic Behavior
is Absent in Children under Three Years
Appears Only Approximately True.

Under each of the examples, give the inferential evidence. Use simple, ordinary language. Do not compress the expression into labels that sound technical and ponderous.

How to write inferential arguments:

1. Place inferential evidence after the specific descriptive evidence it supports.
2. Write hypotheses as timeless generalizations; that is, use present tense.
3. Use a separate heading to reveal each hypothesis and its inferential result. In the heading, express your judgment that an inference is justified. If no inference is justified or if only weak evidence is present, say so.
4. In the space following a heading, give the evidence for a hypothesis (inferential statistics or other inferential evidence).
5. Use interpretive language that is weighted by the strength of the evidence. If you believe the evidence is commanding, say so, but avoid overstating the case. Let good judgment and modesty govern your language, but do not let these requirements keep you from making interpretations for your readers. You can at least say that the *direction* of the evidence agrees or disagrees with your hypothesis.
6. Separately under each hypothesis, organize different lines of inferential evidence, with the most important first. Subordinated headings should precede each separate line of evidence.
7. Never repeat any of the data evidences. Choose one and only one form of presentation: a table, a figure, or ordinary text.
8. Place all related information together so that readers will not have to jump around to understand your intentions.

Calculating and Reporting Confidence Intervals to Justify Inferences

One of the best ways to show the strength of an inference is to place a parameter within a confidence interval and report it in your results. Considering how simple it is to calculate confidence intervals, it is surprising how few investigators report them as evidence. Confidence intervals can be constructed for many different statistics. Use them.

A confidence interval for a correlation coefficient. To see the effectiveness of confidence intervals, consider a correlation between two variables, X and Y, and assume the sample coefficient to be $r_{xy} = .63$. Since the coefficient .63 is a sample estimate of the relation of X to Y, readers will wonder what the population value is [ρ (rho), the symbol for a population parameter]. You can report what the population correlation is likely to be, given the sample estimate and its degrees of freedom. For the calculating procedure, see the index of a text on inferential statistics, such as Minium (1978) or Shavelson (1988).

Now, assume that you have proceeded through the simple calculations and are ready to report the result. The confidence interval should be written in text to look like this:

$$\text{CI}_p \ [.56 \le \rho_{xy} \le .70] = .99$$

You read the confidence interval as follows:

(a) Outside the brackets, CI_p means "confidence interval probability"; at the opposite end, $= .99$ means "has a probability of .99."

(b) Within the brackets, ρ, the population correlation, has a .99 probability (almost complete certainty) of being found within lower and upper limits of $r_{xy} = .56$ and .70.

You can see that such a result is basis for high confidence at $p = .99$, that the degree of relation is moderate (in the narrow band approximately between .56 and .70).

To report a correlation together with its confidence interval, you need only insert the statement within text with words something like the following: The correlation was $r_{xy} = .63$, moderately positive as I anticipated; its parameter is likely to be found within a confidence interval:

$$\text{CI}_p \ [.56 \le \rho_{xy} \le .70] = .99$$

A confidence interval for a difference between two means. Suppose that two drugs, X and Y, have been used to treat a certain disease, and the hours it takes body temperature to return to normal is a criterion of successful treatment. Suppose also that two sample groups of sick people have been treated with one or the other drug. If the mean elapsed time for temperature to reach normal was 10 hours in one group and 12 hours in the other, then the difference was 2 hours. You can construct a confidence interval at $p = .99$ to represent an inference that the difference in effectiveness is within the interval. The end result could look like this:

$$\text{CI}_p \ [.6 \le \mu_x - \mu_y \le 3.4] = .99$$

The probability is .99 in a random variable that the time difference between the two drugs to bring body temperature to normal is somewhere between 0.6 and 3.4 hours.

You are free to construct rows of confidence intervals for a series of statistics, perhaps in a table, but you should report confidence intervals only for those statistics that fit your suppositions. Do not clutter your report with irrelevant information; emphasize only the arguments that relate directly to your suppositions.

Then the confidence interval ($CI_p = .99$) is evidence that the more effective drug will achieve its result anywhere from 0.6 to 3.4 hours sooner than the less effective drug. The advantage of reporting confidence intervals is obvious. The numerals 0.6 and 3.4 are expressed in hours, values in the actual scale of the descriptive variable, and these numerals reflect a range having a probability of .99. The usual inferential statistics are abstract; they do not use numbers from the actual variable (0.6 to 3.4 hours).

Confidence intervals unquestionably make the best inferential arguments from statistics because:

1. The magnitudes at the limits of the intervals are numbers from an actual scale of a variable (for example, if the variable is heart or pulse rate, the numbers making up the confidence interval are in that scale of the real variable—for instance, 65 (lower limit) and 140 (upper limit) are numbers representing heart rates from 65 to 140).

2. They contain a probability for a range (an interval). The probability then has a tangible referent to the variable, which makes the meaning of the probability clear. Other probabilities have more abstract referents.

3. Many inferential statistics can be represented in confidence intervals. In addition to those illustrated in the foregoing section, see Example 3 among the seven examples for reporting statistical analyses that appear in the second half of this chapter. Example 3 is a two-way analysis of variance with planned comparisons (given as confidence intervals).

When Descriptive and Inferential Evidence Is Given Together

Correlation coefficients are descriptive indexes, as are means and standard deviations. Because correlations have easily identified probabilities, they can function as both descriptive and inferential statistics when their probabilities are reported with them. Tables of correlations shown in a report describe degrees of relationship between variables and should be accompanied by a column of *p*-values to allow inferences to their populations. The principle of requiring description first is not violated because both descriptive and inferential arguments appear together in the same display (a table or regular text).

In any of those special kinds of research where descriptive data are accumulated over a long period of time with no intention to test suppositions, it is sometimes possible to give probabilities with them (two-tailed probabilities). Again, the principle of giving the description first is kept intact.

No Intruding Information Belongs in Results

Results chapters are reserved for results; nothing else belongs there. What, then, are results, and how are they distinguished from other text? Results are no more than the data evidences that respond to suppositions. Think of a problem as what was explained in Chapters 2 and 3; think of results as a response to the specific problem you identified in an introduction to your study. Responding to a problem does not mean giving the complete and final answer to the problem; it only means reporting evidence you were able to gather for or against suppositions you have offered.

Nothing about method belongs in a results section.   That means none of the evidence to validate methods used in a study should appear in results. This applies to evidence about reliability or validity of measures. Do not include in a results section evidences to show that assumptions (statistical or other) have been met; these belong in a method section. For example, do not place evidence under results that an assumption of straight-line regression or of homogeneous variance has been satisfied. Place these tests of assumptions in the method section, where the statistical analysis is treated.

Suppose you are ready to write a results section. You wonder how you should begin. Then you recall that not everything in your study worked out exactly as you planned. You may be tempted to start by describing these difficulties and then explain why you think the study is still valid. But you should not do this in the results section.

All these issues are aspects of method that went wrong to some degree. When a *subjects* section is treated in method, you should report the subjects actually studied. If the subject pool is small, you might say in method that a larger pool of subjects was selected but was not included because some failed to

---

What belongs in results:

1. Primary evidence for or against a supposition (a supposition placed in an introduction to the study). This evidence is descriptive.
2. Secondary evidence for or against that same supposition. This evidence is inferential.

What does *not* belong in results:

1. Reliability evidence
2. Validity evidence
3. Tests of statistical assumptions
4. Loss of subjects or other unexpected threats to the validity of the study
5. Statistical or sampling designs
6. Anything procedural involved in carrying out the study

follow instructions. There is little point in making such excuses. In any event, none of these difficulties of procedure belong in a results section.

Similarly, do not outline your statistical design in results.   Explain how your data were analyzed in a method section; the most effective placement for design of data analysis is with *subjects,* as a subsection of method. For example, in the various forms of analysis of variance, a subject pool is partitioned into factors and levels of factors. It is best for readers to see the distribution of subjects at the same time they see the form of analysis. Readers will get a clear picture of an investigator's strategy when related information is placed together in a method section.

Incidental but Interesting Findings

You may come upon some finding that plays no part in any of your lines of evidence but is nonetheless of interest to you and possibly to others. Should you report it? Unless that finding is relevant to your problem, the answer is no. Place the most important evidence first—for example, the best evidence on the most important supposition. Continue with evidence of successively lesser importance. When you have reported all the evidence for your suppositions, conclude the results section.

FORMATS FOR REPORTING VARIOUS STATISTICAL ANALYSES

Example formats for the following categories will be described in this section:

1. Single-classification analysis of variance (ANOVA)
2. Multiple-classification analysis of variance
3. Multiple-classification ANOVA with planned comparisons
4. Multiple regression analysis
5. Discriminant function analysis
6. Multivariate analysis of variance
7. Chi-square analysis

The subject matters for these examples were chosen for their concreteness and the ease with which the examples can be understood. No effort was made to create acceptable research problems to underlie the examples; they are not instances generally of well-chosen problems. With the exception of Example 7, chi-square analysis, which is based on real data, pay no attention to the substance, and give no weight to the outcomes. Each example was written to give readers ideas about organization of results (for example, primary descriptive evidence before secondary inferential evidence; ideas for wording of text, headings, table titles, and figure captions; and ideas about the forms for reporting statistical evidence). *Remember, of the following, only Example 7 is based on real data; none of the other results are to be taken seriously.*

1. A Single-Classification Analysis of Variance

When there are more than two levels of a single independent variable and only one dependent variable, analysis of variance (ANOVA) is used to infer at least one mean difference among the levels.

Scenario: Suppose for this example that you are the investigator, wishing to determine if differences on a final examination having 100 items can be produced by three strategies for teaching introductory statistics. The three strategies are (a) lecture-only, (b) lecture–discussion, and (c) lecture–discussion–computer applications. You have three treatment groups ($N_1 = N_2 = N_3 = 40$).

Your hypothesis is that students do best on a final examination in statistics who get lectures with discussions and computer applications. You also have a hypothesis that students who get lectures with some discussion do better than students who only listen to a lecture.

Form of the written results.   The evidence for these hypotheses is given by descriptive and inferential statistics. What follows is wording and a table to illustrate form for giving results of single-classification ANOVA. The illustration gives wording that can be used when evidences *do not* support a hypothesis. A heading with negative results has been created to illustrate. If you wish, the descriptive evidence can follow immediately after the heading, "Results," or the presentation of both descriptive and inferential evidences can be given as they are in Example 1, under an appropriate heading.

Example 1: Single-Class ANOVA

Results

My Hypotheses Have Not Been Supported:
Condition C Was Not Convincingly
Superior to the Other Methods,
nor Was Condition B Statistically Superior
to Condition A.

Table 5.2 includes mean number of items correct and standard deviations (SD) for three treatment conditions on the 100-point statistics final examination. Notice the similarity of mean scores by the treatment groups.

TABLE 5.2   Means and Standard Deviations on a 100-Point Final Examination for Each of Three Treatment Groups

TREATMENT GROUP	MEAN	SD
Lecture only (A)	87.450	7.670
Lecture–discussion (B)	89.600	7.500
Lecture–discussion–computer applications (C)	91.000	6.535

An analysis of variance has shown that no difference can be inferred in the *populations of the three conditions:*

$$F_{(2/117)} = .785, p = .514$$

What to notice in Example 1:

1. A heading has given away the results before readers see the data evidences.
2. The text has interpretation to direct readers to the important evidence, for example, "Notice the similarity of mean scores."
3. Descriptive statistics (Table 5.2) are given before inferential statistics [$F_{(2/117)} = .785$, $p = .514$].

2. A Two-Way Analysis of Variance (Multiple-Class)

Scenario: Assume that you were not involved in Example 1 but that you are now involved in testing differences among the same three treatments as those in Example 1, strategies for teaching statistics ($N_1 = N_2 = N_3 = 40$). In addition, for the present problem, you are considering the effects of a second independent variable, students who have studied algebra within the past two years versus students whose algebra study goes back more than two years ($N_1 = N_2 = 60$). Scores on the same 100-point final examination continue to be the dependent variable.

You also hold the same two hypotheses as in Example 1 and, as one other hypothesis, you expect students who have studied algebra within the past two years to outperform students whose algebra study goes back more than two years (in sum, three hypotheses). The two hypotheses about teaching strategy will be tested in *one main effect,* and the hypothesis about recent algebra study will be tested in a *second main effect* from a *two-factor analysis of variance.*

Form of the written results.   Examples 1 and 2 illustrate different placements for a first heading after the heading "Results." In Example 2, we will give the descriptive evidences *before* introducing a heading that has an inference in it. It is up to you as the writer whether to give descriptive data before an interpretive heading or to place both descriptive and inferential data after a heading that bears an inference. Either method is satisfactory, and no rule exists to govern the choice.

Example 2: Multiple-Class ANOVA

Results

Descriptive evidences are displayed in Table 5.3 and include means and standard deviations from the statistics examination. Notice that the differences among teaching strategies appear minor, but differences between the two algebra groups are 13 percent of the total test. The relatively large difference between strategy (C), with recent algebra (96.00) and the two strategies (a and b) with distant algebra (77.35 and 79.70, respectively), leads one to suspect an interaction in the populations for teaching strategy and recency of algebra.

TABLE 5.3 Mean Examination Scores and Standard Deviations Associated with Three Teaching Strategies and Recency of Algebra Study

RECENCY OF EXPOSURE TO COLLEGE ALGEBRA	THREE TEACHING STRATEGIES			
	(A)	(B)	(C)	TOTAL
Within two years:				
Mean	87.55	89.00	96.00	90.85
SD	7.00	6.50	5.85	6.45
More than two years:				
Mean	77.35	79.70	76.90	77.98
SD	9.45	10.00	9.80	9.75
Total	82.45	84.35	86.45	84.42
	8.22	8.25	7.82	8.10

Neither Hypothesis about Teaching Strategies Has Much Support from the Analysis.

As you see in Table 5.4, a main effect of teaching strategies is unconvincing ($p = 0.118$). That result could have been anticipated from the small mean differences in total scores relative to the standard deviations (Table 5.3).

There Is Strong Support for the Hypothesis that Recent College Algebra Improves Statistics Performance.

Table 5.4 provides convincing evidence of a final examination difference favoring recent algebra study ($p = .000001$). Although I anticipated a difference in the direction that occurred, its magnitude is greater than I expected.

There Is A Convincing Interaction between Teaching Strategy and Recency of Exposure to College Algebra.

An interaction shown in Table 5.4 ($p = .017$), is interpretable, although I had no hypothesis for it. Figure 5.1 shows that interaction. Note the size of the difference

TABLE 5.4 Sources of Variance Due to Teaching Strategies, Recency of Algebra Study, and Their Interaction

VARIANCE SOURCE	df	MS	F	p
Algebra recency	1	4,588.03	93.63	.000001
Teaching strategy	2	106.63	2.18	.118
Recency × strategy	2	207.43	4.23	.017
Within-cells error	114	49.00		

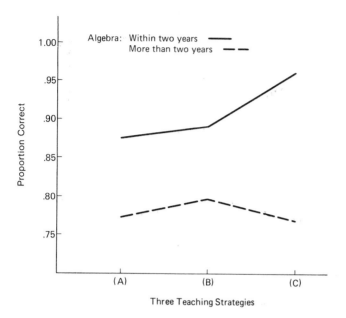

FIGURE 5.1.   On a statistics final examination, an interaction between recency of algebra study and three strategies for teaching statistics [F (2/14) = 4.23, p = .017].

between algebra groups under strategy (C): lecture, discussion, and computer applications. The difference under strategy (C) related to algebra study is approximately twice the size of differences under strategies (A) and (B).

That difference favoring recent algebra study agrees with Peterson's (1989 fictitious) investigation of relations between recent study of algebra and laboratory speed and accuracy in computer-based data analysis. Peterson found that students without any algebra background were the slowest and least accurate of the subjects of her study. She also found a correlation of r_{xy} = .38 between speed of performance in her statistics laboratory and time since algebra was studied.

What to notice in Example 2:

1. In the first paragraph, the text indicates a 13 percent difference separating the algebra groups, and points to interaction.
2. There is complete wording in Table 5.3; the title has both dependent and independent variables. Notice the simple, concrete wording in all headings. Abbreviations are avoided except in column heads.
3. The statistics in Table 5.3 are all given to the same number of decimal places. Whether to provide totals for rows and columns is your choice; totals were included here in the belief that they make it easier to study main effects.
4. An unfavorable outcome was acknowledged in the heading beginning ''Neither hypothesis . . .''

5. In Table 5.4, a variance source table, the title is simple and complete. Probabilities are given as actual calculations ($p =$). Notice the probability favoring algebra recency ($p = .000001$). Sources of variance are given as words, *not abbreviated.*

6. The text interprets Table 5.4 in words like "convincing evidence"; "its magnitude is greater than I expected"; "interaction . . . is interpretable, although I had no hypothesis for it."

7. The reference to Peterson (1989, fictitious) is the author's choice. Place a reference here for emphasis, or place it in discussion. The reference is placed here because the Peterson study is harmonious with the interaction at strategy (C).

8. Figure 5.1 shows a statistical interaction. When interactions occur, they should be graphed and shown in a figure unless an investigator has no interest in that interaction.

9. Figure captions, unlike table titles, are placed at the bottom of figures. Make the captions long enough to communicate what is in the figure. Check a style manual for proper form.

10. In the legend, the writer codes one of the variables (here, algebra was placed in a legend):

Algebra: Within two years = _____

More than two years = ...

3. A Two-Way Analysis of Variance with Planned Comparisons among Means of an Independent Variable

When a study has a rationale with certain hypotheses to be tested, then inferential statistics should be calculated only for those comparisons needed to satisfy the hypotheses. Usually, a study results in more descriptive statistics than will be analyzed inferentially to satisfy hypotheses. The selection of those statistics on which to base inferences is called *planned comparisons* (sometimes these tests are called *a priori tests)*. Comparisons are planned before data collection and calculated after one of the forms of ANOVA. For an example, see Minium (1978, pp. 416–421) or Shavelson (1988, pp. 420–431).

When there are more than two levels of a single independent variable, an F-test (ANOVA) gives only a probability for the largest difference among all the possible mean differences in that variable (including combinations of mean differences). Suppose, for example, there are five levels of an independent variable. Then there are ten differences among the five means. An F-test gives the probability for the largest of these ten differences but no probability for the other nine. Planed comparisons should then be made to test only those differences relevant to hypotheses.

Scenario: Assume, for Example 3, the same hypotheses based on a 100-point final examination as in Example 2. Following ANOVA in Example 3, however, *assume that convincing differences have appeared for both main effects, but no statistical interaction has appeared.*

The hypotheses for Example 3 are: (a) that students experiencing lecture-discussion–computer applications do best on the statistics examination; (b) that students getting lecture and discussion do better than those getting lecture only; and (c) that recent algebra study has advantages over distant algebra for students taking a statistics examination.

Had there been no hypotheses, this study would have called for unplanned comparisons, also called a posteriori comparisons. A study not based on hypotheses will have ANOVA followed by an a posteriori comparison of mean differences (such as a Scheffe test). Most statistics texts refer to these a posteriori comparisons, also called post hoc contrasts. Presentation of unplanned comparisons is similar to that of planned comparisons; they follow analysis of variance.

Form of the written results. The order for reporting the results will be the same as in Example 2. After the ANOVA, usually reported using a variance source table, the planned comparisons between means should be given. These comparisons are important to the inferential analysis because they give the results that respond directly to an investigator's hypotheses.

Example 3: ANOVA with Planned Comparisons

Results

Descriptive evidences are displayed in Table 5.5 and include means and standard deviations on the statistics examination. Final examination results were consistent with both hypotheses about teaching strategies. Compared to a lecture-only group, there was better test performance from a group that discussed statistics given in a lecture, and still better test performance from a lecture group that discussed statistics and also practiced in a computer laboratory. The computer laboratory group correctly answered 11 percent more items than did the group exposed to lecture only.

The descriptive evidence was also consistent with a hypothesis that recent study of algebra enhances the study of statistics. Students who had studied algebra

TABLE 5.5 Mean Examination Scores and Standard Deviations Associated with Three Teaching Strategies and Recency of Algebra Study

RECENCY OF EXPOSURE TO COLLEGE ALGEBRA	THREE TEACHING STARATEGIES			
	(A)	(B)	(C)	TOTAL
Within two years:				
Mean	87.55	92.00	98.80	92.78
SD	6.00	6.50	6.25	6.25
More than two years:				
Mean	77.35	80.50	86.80	81.55
SD	5.25	4.51	5.00	4.92
	82.45	86.25	92.80	87.17
Total	5.62	5.50	5.62	5.58

not more than two years prior to the study of statistics answered correctly 12 percent more items than did students whose algebra study was more than two years old.

The Evidence Favors All Three Hypotheses.

Table 5.6 is a variance source table resulting from analysis of variance. Although the sample sizes were moderate ($n = 40$ for teaching strategies and $n = 60$ for recency of algebra), the differences are highly convincing in both variables. There is no evidence for a statistical interaction between the independent variables.

Planned Comparisons
as Confidence Intervals

Group C versus groups A and B.   The advantage of discussion plus use of a computer laboratory over a composite of the other two methods for teaching statistics is shown below by the $p = .99$ interval of confidence. In this confidence interval, the group exposed to discussion plus computer practice (group C) was compared to the weighted average of the other two groups (A and B). The standard error of this comparison is 1.09. Confidence is high that an advantage on the final examination favoring group C is somewhere between 6 and 11 points.

$$CI_p \left[5.60 \leq \mu_c - \left(\frac{\mu_A + \mu_B}{2} \right) \leq 11.30 \right] = .99$$

Group B versus group A.   Similarly, discussion of statistics hold an advantage over no discussion. The standard error of this comparison is 1.26 examination points. Confidence is $p = .99$ that an advantage on the final examination favoring discussion lies between 0.50 and 7.10 test items.

$$CI_p \left(0.50 \leq \mu_B - \mu_A \leq 7.10 \right) = .99$$

Recent algebra versus distant algebra.   The advantage on the final examination for recent algebra lies somewhere between 8 and 14 points at a probability of .99. The standard error for this comparison is 1.02.

$$CI_p \left(8.56 \leq \mu_R - \mu_D \leq 13.90 \right) = .99$$

TABLE 5.6   Sources of Variance Due to Teaching Strategies, Recency of Algebra Study, and Their Interaction

VARIANCE SOURCE	df	MS	F	p
Algebra recency	1	3,785.63	119.43	.00004
Teaching strategy	2	1,096.43	34.59	.0003
Recency × strategy	2	8.63	.27	.762
Within-cells error	114	31.70		

What to notice in Example 3:

1. The main points of Examples 1 and 2 apply to Example 3: (a) descriptive statistics are given first as the first line of evidence; (b) headings organize the results, are complete, and are easy to understand; (c) headings give away the results; (d) the text is interpretive; it says enough to guide a reader through the results; (e) table titles and headings are written to give complete information; and (f) probabilities are given as equalities to show the degree of convincingness for an inference.

2. Example 3 is here to illustrate a format for presenting planned comparisons as an inferential method of statistical analysis. As the name suggests, planned comparisons are those an investigator anticipates in a hypothesis before obtaining data.

3. Calculations of comparisons are carried out *after* analysis of variance. The F-statistic and its probability apply only to the largest difference among possible differences. Planned comparisons give the probabilities for those differences that are relevant to the study (those planned).

4. Planned comparisons expressed as confidence intervals have special advantages. Each has its own probability, and each confidence interval yields numbers in the actual scale of a variable. In Example 3, you see in the last confidence interval the number 8.56; this number is the lower limit of an interval, but it is also a number relevant to the final examination in statistics. It means 8.56 points of difference on the final examination.

4. A Multiple Regression Analysis

Multiple regression analysis can be used to determine if predictable relations exist between independent variables and a single dependent variable. In Example 4, we are interested in determining the power of two sets of independent variables (also called predictor variables) to predict variation in a dependent variable. See Pedhazur (1982) or Mosteller and Tukey (1977) for various forms and applications of multiple regression analysis.

Scenario: Suppose we hold a theory that leads us to believe that we can predict the amount of depression in a certain segment of the population from our knowledge of seven variables. The seven variables are in two sets; the first set is composed of four demographic variables and the second set of three psychosocial variables. The demographic variables include: (a) years of education, (b) age of the subject, (c) employment status, and (d) annual household income in net dollar amounts. The psychological and sociological variables have been taken as three indexes: (e) a life control index (the degree of control a person believes he or she has over his or her own affairs), (f) a personal accomplishment index, and (g) an index of the extent of a social network supporting a person. We hope that from these seven variables we can predict the number of depression symptoms exhibited by a subject, which will in consequence lend support to our theory about the causes of depression.

Form of the written results. Suppose, then, that we have regressed the magnitude of depression symptoms (our dependent variable) on the two sets of independent variables for a sample of 499 women. We expect evidence for three hypotheses and will organize a results section under headings for these hypotheses. A report of results from regression analysis will have the customary two parts, descriptive and inferential evidences.

Example 4: Multiple Regression Analysis

Results

Means and standard deviations appear in Table 5.7 for four demographic and three psychosocial independent variables, and for depression symptoms as a dependent variable. Intercorrelations among independent variables are given in Table 5.8, along with associated probabilities less than or equal to .10.

TABLE 5.7 Means and Standard Deviations for Demographic and Psychosocial Independent Variables and for Depression as a Dependent Variable

VARIABLES	MEAN	SD
Demographic predictors:		
Years of education	15.37	2.46
Age	29.56	4.58
Employment status	32.45	8.90
Annual household income	20,005.63	1,461.57
Psychosocial predictors:		
Life control index	15.59	5.42
Accomplishment index	39.35	7.68
Social support index	50.50	13.25
Dependent variable:		
Depression symptoms	34.48	5.75

Note: Measures were based on $N = 499$.

TABLE 5.8 Intercorrelations of Demographic (1–4) and Psychosocial (5–7) Independent Variables

VARIABLES	1	2	3	4	5	6	7
1. Years of education	—						
2. Age	.05	—					
3. Employment status	.62	.00	—				
	(.001)						
4. Annual household income	.44	.37	−.11	—			
	(.001)	(.002)	(.080)				
5. Life control	.25	.46	.16	.11	—		
	(.018)	(.001)	(.075)	(.100)			
6. Accomplishment	.36	.47	.22	.21	.53	—	
	(.002)	(.001)	(.016)	(.015)	(.001)		
7. Social support	.18	−.06	−.06	.16	.02	.31	—
	(.070)			(.081)		(.004)	

Note: Probabilities less than or equal to .100 are given in parentheses beneath each associated correlation.

Table 5.8 has intercorrelations among the seven independent variables. The strongest correlation occurred between employment status and education ($r = .62$); more extensive education was associated with higher levels of employment status. Age was moderately correlated with annual household income ($r = .37$) and with accomplishment ($r = .47$). Older women reported higher incomes and greater feelings of accomplishment. Within the psychosocial variables, the strongest relation was between perceived personal control over life situations and personal accomplishment ($r = .53$). The greater were subjects' feelings of control, the greater were their perceived accomplishments. One can interpret that, with some exceptions, there is moderate intercorrelation among the seven variables.

Support Was Found for a Hypothesis that Number of Depression Symptoms Is Associated with the Three Psychosocial Variables.

Table 5.9 has correlations showing associations between the three psychosocial variables and the criterion measure, depression symptoms. All of these correlations appear to be generalizable to a population of women like those of my sample. Although I used measures that were different from those of Warren and McEachren (1995), they found similar relations.

TABLE 5.9 Correlations between Depression Symptoms and Three Psychosocial Variables

VARIABLES	r	p
Social support	$-.298$	.018
Accomplishment	$-.498$	.005
Life control	$-.589$	.001

Partial Support Was Found for a Hypothesis that Depression Symptoms Associate with Certain Demographic Variables.

The correlations between the four demographic variables and depression symptoms are in Table 5.10. Young age, limited education, and low income all appear to be slightly but reliably associated with depression. Contrary to what was expected, symptoms of depression were not related to employment status in the sample.

TABLE 5.10 Correlations between Depression Symptoms and Four Demographic Variables

VARIABLES	r	p
Age	$-.178$	.048
Educational level	$-.278$	.035
Annual household income	$-.249$	.037
Employment status	.010	.966

Support Was Found for a Hypothesis that Psychosocial Variables Are More Strongly Associated with Depression Symptoms than are Demographic Variables

Table 5.11 is the result of hierarchical regression analysis. The analysis was conducted with three sets of variables: (a) 4 demographic variables, (b) 3 psychosocial variables, and (c) 11 interaction variables. The interactions were composed of subsets both within and across the two sets of independent variables. Within sets, the independent variables were entered simultaneously, as suggested by previous researchers and according to theory [appropriate citations]. These interactions were included to determine if one or more combinations of variables would convincingly improve predictions of depression symptoms.

As hypothesized, the set of psychosocial variables convincingly accounted for more variance in depression symptoms (28 percent) than did the set of demographic variables (11 percent), $F(4/471) = 59.588$, $p = .003$. When all three sets of variables, including the 11 interaction variables, were entered into the analysis, their combined relation to depression symptoms was $R^2 = .42$. The 18 variables accounted for 42 percent of the variance in depression symptoms.

TABLE 5.11   Hierarchical Regression of Depression Symptoms on Demographic and Psychosocial Variables and Their Interactions

STEP	VARIABLES ENTERED	INCREMENT IN R^2	F	p
1	4 demographic	.110	90.171	.003
2	3 psychosocial	.281	238.309	.00001
3	11 interaction	.031	2.150	.118

What to notice in Example 4:

1. Descriptive statistics appear first. In the various kinds of correlation studies, descriptive statistics are means, standard deviations, proportions, and correlation coefficients. Only those descriptors that play a part in the argument need to be given in results. All appear in the present study.

    When probabilities are shown with correlation coefficients, the coefficients then serve both a descriptive and an inferential purpose.

2. The meaning of the tables is as independent of the text as I could make them. Study the table titles and heads. Are they complete, and is their wording simple?

3. Intercorrelations among independent variables are important to provide in a multiple regression study because independent variables tend to be interrelated (a disadvantage). Table 5.8 shows how interrelated these variables are.

4. Tables 5.9 and 5.10 give the simple correlations between predictors and the criterion.

5. Table 5.11 shows the progressive improvement in the prediction of a criterion as variables were added to the calculation of multiple correlation (R^2).

6. Notice that results were again interpreted in headings.

5. A Discriminant Function Analysis

In discriminant analysis, one uses several predictor variables to predict a category of best fit for certain objects. In the simplest of examples, we may predict one of two categories: objects that will sell or objects that will not sell; objects that will fit in a container or objects that will not fit; people who will succeed at a task or people who will not succeed. Discriminant analysis can be used to predict more than two classes.

Can a certain manufacturer predict in his inventory which items are likely to be sold by year's end? Suppose buyers respond to variables like the visual attractiveness of an object, the object's size, a mechanical characteristic of the object, its weight, and the like. If each of these characteristics varies from object to object, and each characteristic is more or less attractive to buyers of the objects, then such variables can be considered predictor variables. On the basis of the individual and collective characteristics of the objects, we will estimate which objects will be sold and which will not. This is a statistical scheme by which to use certain known attributes of objects to place the objects in classes: will be sold, will not be sold.

Scenario: Suppose, in Example 5, that you chair a university department and wish to anticipate whether applicants to your undergraduate program are going to be successful in completing the requirements for graduation. To succeed, these students must maintain a cumulative grade point average (GPA) of at least 2.00 (C). Those candidates whose average grades are equal to or greater than 2.00 will be classified as successful. Those who do not maintain a 2.00 cumulative GPA will be classified as unsuccessful.

The faculty want students to succeed. They know it is stressful and expensive for students to fail, and the quality of instruction for other students suffers as well. Although more than half of the faculty are skeptical about the prospects of improving the department's prediction of student success, the faculty decide to do a discriminant analysis to see if they can correctly anticipate who will succeed among applicants for study.

The department has been collecting basic information on each of its applicants and then, on the basis of that information, has made subjective judgments to admit certain students. Included in that information are three of the best predictor variables identified in past research: (a) Scholastic Aptitude Test (SAT) verbal scores, (b) SAT quantitative scores, and (c) an interviewer's ratings. Although individually these predictors have helped the faculty to make admission decisions, they have not permitted the faculty to identify the potentially successful student.

Nevertheless, a combination of the same three continuous predictor variables (independent variables) is now to be used to classify students as likely to succeed or not succeed; this is a circumstance for discriminant analysis. If the discriminant analysis classifies those applicants as likely to succeed who actually do later succeed, then in the future discriminant analysis may be a basis for the actual decisions to admit students.

Form of the written results.   The evidence for the discriminating power of the three variables is given by descriptive and inferential statistics, in that order as usual. The illustration that follows gives wording and tables that show how discriminant analysis can be presented. The use of headings to separate results into two sections is not always necessary. The division was done here to make clear that there are two parts to the analysis: (a) the classification of students as succeeding or not succeeding, together with results showing how many of the predictions were correct (data analysis), and (b) the discriminant function equations to be used for future classifications of new applicants (future use depends on discriminant analysis identifying the successful students).

Example 5: Discriminant Function Analysis

Results

Table 5.12 includes mean scores on both SAT measures and interviewer's ratings for two groups, those with satisfactory grades and those without. Notice the higher test scores and interview ratings earned by successful students on all three measures; the largest difference in scores occurred on the SAT quantitative test. Note also the larger standard deviations for the unsuccessful students on the quantitative measure and the interview rating.

In Table 5.13, I have presented the results of discriminant analysis. There are large discrepancies between successful and unsuccessful candidates on all

TABLE 5.12 Mean Scores and Standard Deviations from Three Predictor Variables (SAT Verbal, SAT Quantitative, and Interviewer Rating) Obtained from Undergraduate Students Whose Scholarship Was Successful or Unsuccessful

STUDENTS MEETING, NOT MEETING A SCHOLARSHIP CRITERION	THREE PREDICTOR VARIABLES		
	SAT VERBAL	SAT QUANTITATIVE	INTERVIEWER RATING
Successful (GPA $\geq$ 2.00):			
Mean	627.55	580.00	88.50
SD	37.00	66.50	15.50
Unsuccessful (GPA $<$ 2.00):			
Mean	567.00	491.00	69.25
SD	31.66	75.50	21.00

Note: SAT = Scholastic Aptitude Test; GPA = grade point average.

TABLE 5.13 Classification/Confusion Matrices from Discriminant Analysis of Three Predictor Variables for Two Groups of Students, Those Meeting and Those Not Meeting a GPA Criterion

ACTUAL GROUP	PREDICTED GROUP MEMBERSHIP		
	NUMBER OF CASES	(1)	(2)
GPA $\geq$ 2.00 (1)	50	50 (1.000)	0 (0.000)
GPA $<$ 2.00 (2)	50	2 (0.040)	48 (0.960)

three predictor variables. Those three variables gave perfect predictions of which students would meet the GPA criterion and gave 96 percent accurate predictions of which students would not meet the GPA criterion.

Table 5.14 includes unstandardized and standardized coefficients from the discriminant function analysis. The resulting discriminant function, based on a sample of 100 students who have completed baccalaureate studies, is: $D = 0.6593Z_1 + 0.5796Z_2 + 0.9750Z_3$ (1)

$$\text{where } Z_1 = \text{SAT verbal scores}$$
$$Z_2 = \text{SAT quantitative scores}$$
$$Z_3 = \text{interview rating score}$$

Since the coefficients are standardized, one can conclude that interviewers' ratings and SAT verbal scores are more important than SAT quantitative scores in classifying applicants as likely to succeed or not succeed.

TABLE 5.14   Unstandardized and Standardized Discriminant Function Coefficients

	UNSTANDARDIZED	STANDARDIZED
Z_1	.3608	.6593
Z_2	2.6119	.5796
Z_3	.5303	.9750
Constant	12.8968	

We use discriminant analysis when:

1. We want to classify items, objects, or observations into two or more mutually exclusive groups.
2. We have continuous variables serving as predictors.
3. We have taken discriminant functions and their equations from one sample and wish to use those same equations to predict or classify new objects from a new and different sample.

Show results from discriminant analysis as:

1. A table of descriptive statistics for predictor variables and a criterion variable (like Table 5.12)
2. A tabled matrix of classifications (confusions) to identify the proportion of an original sample correctly classified (like Table 5.13)
3. A table or text to display the discriminant function coefficients (like Table 5.14)

6. A Multivariate Analysis of Variance

Multivariate analysis of variance (MANOVA) is one member of the family of analyses of variance. In that instance where there is more than one dependent variable (criterion variables) and these variables are correlated with each other, a multivariate analysis of variance is an appropriate form of analysis provided that all the ordinary assumptions of analysis of variance can be met.

Scenario: Suppose you are an exercise therapist or exercise physiologist interested in whether the clients with whom you work will improve in physical health as you work with them. Moreover, you have decided that blood pressures should be proper indexes of health, on the assumption that blood pressure relates to the exercise you require of your clients. These blood pressures, taken when a client is at rest, include both systolic pressure and diastolic pressure. The two measures of blood pressure are viewed as separate dependent measures for this example. Further, since there is more than one dependent variable, *and* these dependent variables are known to be highly correlated ($r_{SD} = 0.834$), one MANOVA should be used rather than two separate ANOVAs.

In collecting data on exercise and blood pressure, you have classified 240 female clients into several research classes on the basis of two methods of classification. One classification variable is exercise at two levels: (a) clients who exercise at least three times a week and (b) clients who exercise less often than three times a week. Another classification variable is a measure of fitness based on ideal weight; weight is represented at three levels: (a) weight of clients more than 20 percent below their ideal weight, (b) weight within 20 percent of ideal weight, and (c) weight more than 20 percent above ideal weight.

You have three hypotheses: (a) that those who exercise three or more times a week have lower resting blood pressures, systolic and diastolic, than do those exercising fewer than three times a week; (b) that those at or below their ideal body weights have lower blood pressures than do those judged overweight; and (c) that there is an interaction between the two independent variables such that greater body weight combined with little exercise produces disproportionately high blood pressures. In summary, you expect two main effects and an interaction at each of systolic pressure and diastolic pressure.

Form of the written results. Examples 1 through 3 illustrate one- and two-way ANOVAs having in each case only one dependent measure or variable. In the MANOVA of Example 6, we will display descriptive and inferential statistics based on two correlated dependent measures, systolic and diastolic blood pressures.

As in Example 1, we will guide readers with a heading placed before descriptive evidences and with headings before the inferential evidences. A writer can judge whether to place an interpretive heading before descriptive data. With multiple dependent variables, however, an early heading organizes descriptive evidences and eases interpretation for a reader.

Example 6: MANOVA

Results

Blood Pressures at Relative Body Weights

Descriptive statistics are displayed in Table 5.15 and include means and standard deviations for both systolic and diastolic blood pressures for 240 females.

Notice that differences in blood pressures between women in the two exercise categories appear substantial, and lower pressures are associated with higher levels of exercise; the systolic difference was 22.69 and the diastolic difference 18.10. The relative increases in mean blood pressures as one scans across the weight classifications also appear substantial; low body weight is associated with lower blood pressure (from 112.78/83.96 to 149.23/114.91).

TABLE 5.15   Mean Systolic and Diastolic Blood Pressures and Their Standard Deviations That Are Associated with Three Weight Classifications and Two Levels of Physical Exercise

		BODY WEIGHT			
		20% BELOW IDEAL	WITHIN 20% OF IDEAL	20% ABOVE IDEAL	
		Systolic Blood Pressures			Average
3+ Exercises weekly	Mean SD *N*	111.50 11.00 22	119.00 16.50 61	136.00 19.85 37	122.87 16.79
0-2 Exercises weekly	Mean SD *N*	114.35 13.45 18	141.50 18.00 39	157.00 24.80 63	145.56 21.34
Averages		112.78 12.16	127.78 17.10	149.23 23.09	134.22 19.20
		Diastolic Blood Pressures			
3+ Exercises weekly	Mean SD *N*	80.50 9.75 22	89.00 15.50 61	103.00 22.65 37	91.76 17.26 120
0-2 Exercises weekly	Mean SD *N*	88.20 9.45 18	100.40 19.00 39	121.90 29.80 63	109.86 24.43 120
Averages		83.96 9.62	93.45 16.95	114.91 27.37	100.81 21.15

Both Hypotheses Anticipating Main Effects from Exercise and Body Weight Have Been Supported by the Analysis.

Multivariate statistics (Wilks's lambda) and their associated univariate statistics (exact Fs) for both main effects and an interaction are presented in Table 5.16. As you can see in that table, a multivariate main effect for levels of exercise is highly convincing ($p = 0.00001$). That result seems evident in Table 5.15 from the large mean differences in total scores relative to the standard deviations. In addition, the multivariate main effect for varying body weight is also highly convincing ($p = 0.00001$).

A Hypothesis of Interaction between Body Weight and Exercise Was Supported Only at Systolic Pressure.

Multivariate evidence for an interaction is shown in Table 5.16 ($p = .0001$). Interpretation of the interaction is through the univariate Fs, where body weights in the study have interacted with levels of exercise to influence systolic blood pressures ($p = 0.020$), but have not convincingly interacted to effect diastolic pressure ($p = 0.291$). Figure 5.2 illustrates these interactions. In Figure 5.2 systolic pressure progressively separates the two exercise groups as body weight increases. The slopes of the lines for diastolic pressure do not separate the exercise groups sufficiently to make one confident of an interactive influence of body weight and exercise.

TABLE 5.16 **Multivariate and Univariate Sources of Variance in Systolic and Diastolic Blood Pressures Classified According to Body Weight and Amount of Exercise, and Their Interactions**

VARIANCE SOURCE	MULTIVARIATE WILKS'S LAMBDA	df/df	UNIVARIATE MS/MS	EXACT F	p
		Body Weight			
	0.670	4/466		22.754	0.000001
Systolic		2/234	16,746.277 368.640	45.427	0.000001
Diastolic		1/234	13,409.242 447.322	29.977	0.000001
		Physical Exercise			
	0.879	2/233		16.016	0.000001
Systolic		1/234	11,553.562 368.640	31.341	0.000001
Diastolic		1/234	7,765.753 447.322	17.360	0.000001
		Weight × Exercise			
	0.918	4/466		5.108	0.0001
Systolic		1/234	1,475.510 368.640	4.002	0.020
Diastolic		2/234	555.834 447.322	1.242	0.291

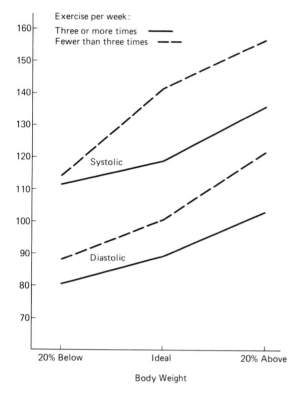

FIGURE 5.2   For systolic blood pressure, an interaction between body weight and frequency of exercise [F (2/234) = 4.00, p = .020]. For diastolic blood pressure,
and unconvincing interaction between body weight and frequency of exercise
[F (2/234) = 1.242, p .291].

What to notice in Example 6:

1. There are two *correlated* dependent variables, systolic and diastolic blood
    pressures. The presence of two or more correlated dependent variables in
    analysis of variance calls for MANOVA—multivariate analysis of variance.

2. Study the headings. Do they correctly anticipate content? The first para-
    graph heading, "Blood Pressures at Relative Body Weights," precedes the
    descriptive indexes. Some people would use no heading or would omit "at
    Relative Body Weights." The heading is, however, purposeful; it does cre-
    ate a correct mind set for a reader, and it presents a complete idea, which
    requires "at Relative Body Weights."

3. When inferential statistics are presented, it is *first* necessary to report a
    multivariate F-ratio. If that multivariate F is too small to convince an inves-
    tigator (a matter of experience and judgment), then univariate F-ratios can-
    not be considered and the study is not a basis for inferences; interpretation

stops there. On tne other hand, when multivariate *F*s are convincing, then one looks next to univariate *F*-ratios. Univariate *F*s are usually the basis for inferences in response to hypotheses.

4. The *F*-ratios in Example 6 are of much greater magnitudes than are found in most research. The probabilities for these *F*-ratios are therefore extremely rare and overwhelmingly convincing. These unusual probabilities are here to illustrate probabilities taken to many decimal places. Convincingness is relative, and the smaller a probability, the more believable the result.

5. Table 5.16 shows sources of variance due to exercise, body weight, and interaction. Such a table is not common in reporting multivariate analysis of variance, but it is an effective way to organize information for readers.

6. A hypothesis of interaction between exercise and body weight was meant to apply to both systolic and diastolic pressures. That hypothesis was supported for systolic pressure but not for diastolic pressure. Just how much damage the partial failure has done to a theory depends on a rationale for the study, which, of course, is in the introduction to the study. The discussion section should also treat failure of the hypothesis.

7. Figure 5.2 shows evidence for two interactions, some interaction in both systolic and diastolic blood pressure. This figure is descriptive evidence, not inferential. The figure caption gives *F*-ratios and probabilities. These statistics are the inferential arguments; one is convincing, one is not. Notice that the caption appears at the bottom of the figure.

8. Confidence intervals for the inferential statistics are missing. Such evidence would improve the multivariate argument, but the intervals were omitted here to save space. It is wise to use confidence intervals; see Example 3 for a general format for confidence intervals.

7. Chi-Square Analysis

Chi-square is a commonly used nonparametric statistic. To determine if relations, also called dependencies, exist among categories within variables, chi-square is a likely form of analysis. The data collected for chi-square are frequencies or counted observations placed in nominal categories; as frequency counts, these data are not usable with the inferential analyses illustrated in Examples 1 through 6. See Fienberg (1980) for an alternative method.

Scenario: Suppose that an investigator in the field of public policy and criminal justice is interested in facts surrounding victims who are the repeated targets of crime. This investigator asks, "Are some people likely to be repeated victims of the same crime?" The investigator thinks so for several reasons and has formed a hypothesis to that effect. However, there are two principal views to be considered, which run through the literature of criminal and victim behavior. One theory holds that after being victimized once, a victim is made aware of circumstances and surroundings for that particular crime and is less likely to fall into those same circumstances. The opposing theory is that some people have predispositions to become victims. These people have enduring habits that make them vulnerable to exploitation by criminals. In this theory, such people remain vulnerable to criminal acts, even after being victimized; that is the basis for the hypothesis in Example 7. If chi-square is large enough to be convincing in Example 7, it will mean that there is a relation between the kind of crime first committed against a person and the kind of crime committed a second time against that same person.

The federal government and state and local authorities keep updated information on victims and the crimes perpetrated against them. These data make possible an empirical attempt to respond to the hypothesis and possibly strengthen one theory while weakening the other. In Example 7, the entire data pool consists of frequencies for the occurrence of a second crime, either identical to the first crime or a different crime committed on the same victim. These are real data obtained from the 1980 National Crime Survey (Reiss, 1980), but the rationale was created here to illustrate chi-square.

The frequencies for a second crime have been classified as one of the following acts: A, assault; B, burglary; HL, household larceny; MV, motor vehicle theft; PL, personal larceny; PT, petty theft; RA, rape; and RO, robbery with a weapon.

Form of the written results.   Frequency counts and proportions are common descriptive statistics (primary data) in chi-square analysis. Depending on the nature of the problem, sometimes median frequencies and an index of variation can be used as descriptors. In Example 7, only frequencies and proportions are the descriptive statistics because no others are needed or relevant. Table 5.17 contains all the descriptive evidence for this example. The inferential statistic is presented very simply within text as a chi-square statistic, its associated degrees of freedom, and its probability. This constitutes the total of the secondary evidence. Be prepared for a surprise in Example 7; chi-square is vastly larger than those one will ordinarily see, and this sample statistic, unlike those in Examples 1 through 6, is based on real data.

Example 7: Chi-Square Analysis*

Results

Frequencies totaling 57,407 for second crimes committed against the same individuals have been subdivided into eight classes representing kinds of crimes first committed against these people; these frequencies are presented in Table 5.17. Proportions appear under the frequencies to represent each of the eight classes displayed across a row. Table 5.17 makes possible a comparison of the kind of crime committed on the first and subsequent occasions. By examining the proportions in Table 5.17, one can see that the same people tend to be victims on repeated occasions of the same crime who were victims on a first occasion.

---

*Example 7 was drawn from a study by Reiss (1980). Although the data in Table 5.17 are the actual data, I created the wording in Example 7 to illustrate certain concepts; investigator Reiss is not responsible for this wording. See Fienberg (1980) for a collection of chi-square examples that illustrate a range of applications of the chi-square method. Anyone analyzing frequency data would do well to study the Fienberg text.

TABLE 5.17   Frequency of the Second of Two Crimes: Same Person Being a Repeat Victim of the Same or a Different Kind of Crime

FIRST OF TWO CRIMES	SECOND OF TWO CRIMES							
	(A)	(B)	(HL)	(MV)	(PL)	(PT)	(RA)	(RO)
Assault	2,997	1,083	1,349	216	2,553	85	65	238
(A)	.349	.126	.157	.025	.297	.010	.008	.028
Burglary	1,117	3,210	1,973	301	2,649	102	52	191
(B)	.116	.335	.206	.031	.276	.011	.005	.020
Household	1,251	1,962	4,646	391	3,757	117	42	206
Larceny (HL)	.101	.159	.376	.032	.304	.009	.003	.017
Motor vehicle	221	301	367	269	678	24	3	51
theft (MV)	.115	.157	.192	.141	.354	.013	.002	.027
Personal	2,628	2,658	3,689	687	12,137	229	75	2628
larceny (PL)	.117	.118	.164	.031	.539	.010	.003	.018
Petty theft	102	115	101	38	243	61	3	40
(PT)	.145	.164	.144	.054	.346	.087	.004	.145
Rape	50	39	48	11	82	6	26	11
(RA)	.183	.143	.176	.040	.300	.020	.095	.040
Robbery	279	197	221	47	459	36	12	197
(RO)	.193	.136	.153	.032	.317	.025	.008	.136
Totals	8,645	9,565	12,394	1,960	22,558	660	278	1,347
	.151	.167	.216	.034	.393	.011	.005	.023

Source: The data in Table 5.17 are from ''Victim Proneness by Type of Crime in Repeat Victimization'' by A. J. Reiss, Jr. in *Indicators of Crime and Criminal Justice: Quantitative Studies,* edited by S. E. Fienberg and A. J. Reiss, Jr. Copyright 1980, Washington, D. C., U.S. Government Printing Office. Adapted by permission.

Proportions were calculated and added to the Reiss data for Table 5.17. These proportions are given with each frequency (for example, in the upper left, of people who have been victimized twice, beginning with assault, .349 of 8 crimes are repeated assaults; in .126 of 8,586 cases, burglary has followed assault on the same victims). A row of proportions equals unity.

Notice, for example, that about one-third of the time, assault, burglary, and household larceny are committed a second time against the same victims. Notice also that repetitions of the same crime occur more often than instances of a different crime. Follow the proportions across the diagonal from upper left to lower right.

A Hypothesis Has Been Supported that People Tend to Be Repeat Victims of the Same Crime.

Chi-square analysis of frequencies in Table 5.17 has yielded a highly convincing statistic showing that the frequencies are not randomly distributed across the eight categories (x^2 (49) = 11,190, p = .0000001). Because the frequencies of second crimes tend to fall often into the same classes as first crimes, I take the evidence as favoring the theory that some people have predispositions to be victims of crime; they tend to be repeat victims of the same class of crime.

What to notice in Example 7:

1. Example 7 required very careful wording so that readers will understand that *all data* evidences are frequencies of second crimes committed against the same individuals. In reporting research, it is not easy to create all of the correct interpretations. Pay close attention to the amount of explanation and interpretation. Results sections need to be complete and sufficient for readers. Choose words and sentences for precision of meaning. Without experience, that is hard to do.

2. Before chi-square analyses, descriptive evidence should be given in the form of frequencies or proportions, or both. In the present study, the primary evidence is easier to interpret in the proportions.

3. The inferential statistic chi-square is almost always given in text, as it is in Example 7.

4. Not all the evidence in Table 5.17 agrees with the hypothesis in the study. Notice in the case of petty theft that repeat victims of that crime occur only with an incidence of .087 (for rape, also, the proportion is small). These contrary cases should be pointed out in the results and dealt with in the discussion section.

CHAPTER 6

How to Write a Discussion

Theses and most research journals provide for a separate discussion section following results. Occasionally, results and discussion are given together. But a discussion section having its own heading and placed separate from results works well because readers can first assimilate the data from the results section before considering an investigator's arguments about the fit of the results to existing beliefs about such phenomena.

CONTENT FOR A DISCUSSION

Open a discussion by telling what you learned, or believe, now that your study is completed. Get right to the point, without unnecessary small talk. A discussion gives the status of a research problem once the data have been analyzed; it tells how believable, in light of the data, your suppositions about the problem are. The discussion also includes your explanatory arguments, which fit the present data to earlier data and theory. Discussions are analytical and interpretive; they fit phenomena to suppositions and, when possible, suppositions to theories.

Limit your discussion to the central ideas of your research, taking those ideas one at a time. Start with what your data appear to show as a generalization (a supposition); call attention to patterns in the data. Tell how others' evidences agree and disagree. Above all, focus your words on the elements of relations between variables and differences within them. Do not simply draw conclusions for your readers; instead, analyze data within variables, pointing out how mechanisms may be operating within those variables. Set out your argument carefully, bit by bit, so that readers get a complete picture of your interpretations. Explain the relations; in the discussion, your watchword is explain.

Respond to questions like these:

1. Was your problem satisfied by the results you obtained? Even if a problem and results agree perfectly, it is unlikely that your problem has been put to rest. Problems have too many ramifications to be satisfied by one study.
2. In what ways was the strategy of your research especially effective in giving you an argument for your interpretation of the data?
3. Have you more than one line of evidence toward the same conclusion?
4. Do the data and theories of other investigators accord with your data and suppositions?
5. What advantage does your interpretation have over other interpretations for integration of your findings with existing belief (knowledge)?
6. What disadvantage does your interpretation have for integrating knowledge? What are the strengths of alternative explanations?

As much as possible, base your interpretations on data. All of your assertions will be questioned, and those with the strongest objective basis will be the easiest for readers to accept. When you have assertions that are some distance from the data, admit it, but use positive and balanced language; avoid apologizing.

Limit the discussion to the final and best state of your thinking—what you understand after you have worked long and hard to put this effort together. A discussion should be positive. Don't recreate in a discussion all the fumbling you may have gone through to get to this point.

Construct an organized interpretation of the research based on that final, postinvestigative set of interpretations. You do research in order to understand and organize; reporting, then, should reflect your understanding at its most satisfactory state. A discussion should not resort to incomplete or unsatisfactory concepts that may have been in your mind in the process of investigating. Focus your discussion; focus it on what you have come to understand and believe.

Conclusions

You may use the word *conclusions* to bring together a summary statement for your discussion. If you do, be cautious in what you draw conclusions about. If the evidences justify it, you can say in conclusion, "My data fit hypothesis A better than any competing hypothesis." Keep in mind, however, that one or two studies are rarely enough to settle controversies or establish suppositions. Belief within a community of scholars changes slowly and progressively. In the social sciences, research seldom leads to a final conclusion in the minds of readers. Let your conclusions show how *relatively* believable they are.

Style and Graphic Auxiliaries

The discussion is a continuation of your introduction. Therefore, the style and content should be similarly explanatory. Method and results have more to do with particulars. On redrafting your thesis, you may find it advantageous to move some of the language back and forth between the introduction and the discussion. Both sections deal with the status of a problem.

Rework what you have written, paring it down to the essential sentences. Be critical of your own logic, and continue reworking the language until you are satisfied that you have made your points. An effective discussion is not necessarily a long discussion; it is one that convinces.

Within a discussion, it is appropriate to use figures to represent abstract concepts, just as you might use them in an introduction. Synthesis, as a theoretical representation of different lines of evidence, is often best given in a figure. A very simple table of another investigator's data may also be helpful if it does not take up much space and if it helps you form an argument.

WRONG CONTENT FOR A DISCUSSION

Discussions require as much rigor as does any other aspect of research and reporting. This is not the place for cavalierly tossing together a few ideas. In one sense, the data speak for themselves, but the data do not organize themselves nor do they assemble themselves into a cogent argument. Assemble your results section in such a way as to make certain interpretations more likely than others. Then, in a discussion following results, thoughtfully put together the arguments that make one interpretation more likely than others. A discussion should not be a potpourri of incidental occurrences during the course of research.

Don't substitute a summary for a discussion.   Students regularly make the mistake of substituting a summary of results for a discussion of them. Summary is the purpose of an *abstract*. (Infrequently, a committee may ask for a separate section called "Summary"; do not create one unless you are asked to do so.) *A discussion is not a restatement of your problem or your results.*

Throughout your thesis, be guided by this principle: Say only once what you intend; don't repeat. Bring everything together that needs to be said, and write that content so well it will not need repeating. When readers arrive at the discussion, they have just finished reading your results. They can remember whatever was clearly stated in your presentation.

Of course, you must point to certain of the results, but do so as simply as you can—for example: "The superiority of A over B was expected [but turned out to be more/less than expected]. Now, why wasn't the difference larger?" The point is that you should refer to a result in a general way, but avoid giving the actual data again. When students summarize in a discussion, they probably do so because they do not know what actually is appropriate to a discussion. Note that the *Publication Manual of the American Psychological Association* (1983, p. 27), says: "Do not, however, simply reformulate and repeat points already made; each new statement should contribute to your position and to the readers' understanding of the problem." *Read and follow the suggestions on pages 27 and 28 of the* APA Manual *and those suggestions in the* Council of Biology Editors Style Manual *(1978, p. 11).*

Don't justify your research by claiming it has practical applications.   A discussion should never be apologetic, and it is not a place to justify research simply because you or others think it has practical ramifications. Remember: Research is justified by what it allows us to understand. When we understand relations between variables, it may then be possible to make practical applications. But why state the obvious? Only if there are applications that readers might miss should you make a point of noting your research's applications. Your discussion will be dull indeed if you fill it with lists of obvious but unlikely applications or create applications that are implausible because you feel compelled to say how your research applies.

Don't make a discussion out of all the little things that went wrong in your study.   Your work will not be valued simply because you admit to a list of failures and think you can explain them away. Accept your work as it was, and then proceed to analyze what can be analyzed. Otherwise, your readers will desert you.

Don't fill up space by listing topics for further research.   So many writers list questions for further research that you may think it necessary to imitate them. Resist this temptation. These lists tend to be impulsively generated and seldom meet the criteria of a discussion. If you have confidence that research related to your original research problem should take some new direction, and you can say why, then of course you should take up that discussion. But don't list topics for future research simply because it is an easy way to fill the space. When you have finished being analytical and interpretive, end your discussion.

Include in a discussion:

1. The postinvestigative status of your research problem. Begin immediately with that status; do not slip into the topic by way of a long series of preliminaries and incidentals.

2. The central point of your problem, namely the postinvestigative status of your suppositions that explain the phenomena you studied. Tell how well your data argue the case of your suppositions. If your study helps to fit the suppositions to existing theory, tell how it does so.

Sources of argument:

1. Refer to variables by name, describing relations between and differences within variables to make your case.

2. Make your interpretations from data; when you go beyond the data, acknowledge it.

3. Point to patterns in the data.

4. Describe mechanisms that may be operating.

4. Tell how your data agree or disagree with others' data. How well do these data sources integrate compared to other interpretations?

6. How effective was your strategy of research? What about it was especially appropriate to the problem?

7. Did your study have more than one line of evidence, each supported by its own data? Did they work together well to force an interpretation?

Omit from a discussion:

1. Incidental findings and ideas

2. A summary (don't repeat your problem statement or your results)

3. Justifications and apologies, such as a claim that the research has practical implications.

4. What went wrong in the research, and what might have happened had this not gone wrong

5. Topics for further research, unless you have a genuine insight and have given the matter careful thought

AN EXAMPLE DISCUSSION

The discussion that follows is based on the Harlow (1971) mother surrogate studies, used in Chapter 3 to illustrate an introduction. Because you are familiar with that introduction and because introductions and discussions have some similarities, that study makes a good example. *Please note that the following discussion was not written by Harlow. It was created here to fit this chapter.* Although the discussion was intended to follow Harlow's interpretations, it is difficult to know whether the interpretations fit his in every detail, particularly the temporal order of events. Harlow had a superb style for discussion. His expressions were highly analytical but clear and simple and therefore interesting even to lay readers. You would do well to adopt a style similar to that of Harlow (1971, pp. 17–28).

Discussion

Visualize two artificial mothers side by side—one cloth-covered, one of bare wire. Then imagine infant monkeys entering a room halfway between the mothers and a frightening mechanical monster moving threateningly, creating noise, and flashing its illuminated eyes. Not only do our data show that the baby monkeys fled unfailingly toward the cloth-covered mother, but those of us observing saw facial signs of genuine fright.

From the frightening object, the infants ran to the cloth mother, taking ventral positions on her and clinging tightly to her. Our motion picture films show, and those who have seen the films agree, that our infant monkeys were initially truly frightened, but as these babies clung to the cloth mother, they gradually were comforted, gave vocal signs of their contentment, and progressively relaxed their fearful grip on the mother. Shortly, they were playing in front of the cloth mother, reassured by her presence.

In a complementary study, when the cloth mother was placed behind a Plexiglas barrier and the frightened monkeys had to run past the mechanical monster to take refuge on the cloth mother, there was easily recognized reticence, perhaps even horror, on the faces of the babies. Nevertheless, all the monkey babies eventually braved the gauntlet, jumped to the cloth mother, clung to her, and looked warily toward the monster.

The Relative Power of Contact Comfort

Although the wire mother had been the sole source of nourishment for certain of the monkey babies, the babies fed by the wire mother appeared to get no comfort from her. The babies made their escape directly to the cloth mother, and only when they were reassured did they go to the wire mother to take the nursing bottle projecting from her. Beyond these research observations is the advertiser's cliché: *You must see to appreciate.* Our films showed singular resort to the cloth mother when monkey babies were frightened, and the babies showed easily recognized signs of relaxation and reassurance as they continued to take contact comfort from her.

Although my associates and I have interpreted that the infant monkeys gave the best evidence of their attachment to the cloth-covered mother when frightened, they demonstrated unequivocal preference for her when not frightened. Contact comfort was a generally powerful force in the attachment of infant monkeys. These monkeys selected an object of comfort, not because it was a source of food but, rather, because it satisfied their basic disposition to cuddle. Not only do the data show that disposition, but the visual episodes are equally convincing.*

Arguments from folklore to formal theory, intended as explanation for an infant's attachment to a mother, have centered on some form of innate drive; generally hunger reduction has been the explanatory mechanism. Bowlby (1969) [Harlow's reference] called it the "cupboard theory." But there have been reasons to ques-

---

*Of course, not every study has motion pictures that one can refer to as a source of evidence. Use whatever evidences you have that are clear and convincing.

tion such a theory. Van Wagenen (1950) [Harlow's reference but not the present author] found that infant monkeys without mothers needed cloth lining in their baskets or they were unable to feed normally. Given cheesecloth pads, they wrapped themselves and became attached to these soft pads. That the soft contact is so important as to overwhelm other variables had not been evident and was, to my colleagues and myself, a surprise.

But what of the absence of reciprocal love? The monkey babies never had their affections returned. Our artificial mothers never caressed their infants, never held them tightly to their breasts, never made maternal sounds. These mothers had only superficial visual qualities of a mother; they never moved or made vocal responses to their babies, but some of these mothers had the redeeming quality of being soft.

Even before a baby is born, a real mother has associations to her infant as it is nestled in the protective bliss of her womb. When the infant is born, the mother fondles it, guarding the baby night and day; a mother's attachment is present at birth. Moreover, the attachments of mothers for babies and babies for mothers are so intertwined that it is a forbidding task to unravel them. How can one know which is a mother-initiated response and which is an infant's response?

When, in the laboratory, my associates and I gave up reciprocal love between a real mother and her infant, losing all the real motherly attributes but reconstituting one attribute by representing it in cloth over wire, we could not anticipate that soft contact would, by itself, be sufficient. We were surprised that the effects of artificial contact comfort proved to be powerful; it attested to the strength of a supposition that bodily contact is a relatively more powerful variable than other variables associated with infant attachment to a mother.

Indeed, the wire mothers made possible the control of variables and resulted in a convincing picture of infantile attachment through contact comfort, just as Thompson's (1963) [Harlow's reference] model of a fish helped to establish belly color as a determining variable in the aggressiveness of the stickleback fish and Hess's (1959) [Harlow's reference] wooden objects permitted the separation of auditory and visual stimuli in explaining certain imprinting phenomena in ducks.

A Differential Response
to an Artificial Mother

In the space of a few hours, our baby monkeys soaked their artificial mothers in urine. Differential responses these were, but not deferential. Other monkey babies do not soil their real mothers, and animals in the wild do not ordinarily even foul their own nests. In that the experimental animals responded so convincingly to the contact surface, spending time there and taking solace in it when threatened, it is puzzling that micturition was not inhibited on the cloth mother. Of course, it is quite possible that real mothers recognize some bodily sign in their babies and have some method of inhibiting urination. Nevertheless, watching real mothers as we did for some sign of maternal control over her infant's bladder, we saw no signaling that we could associate with urination, nor could we reach any reasonable supposition to explain their babies' continence.

A Generalization that Cannot Be Made

One might wonder whether tactile stimulation can be increased or exaggerated beyond that which is normal to the possible benefit of intensifying mother–infant attachment. Studies such as those of Schaffer and Emerson (1964) [Harlow's reference] offer no such hope. These investigators arranged for exaggerated handling of infants by their mothers and for increased talking and smiling in the presence of their infants. The evidence failed to show intensified infant response to the mothers. From all that we have observed in our laboratory, we do not believe that more than normal surface contact has either a beneficial effect on normal infants or a remedial effect on autistic monkey infants that have been at first deprived of contact comfort.

Influence Other Than Contact Comfort on Infantile Attachment

In spite of the power of contact comfort, a study by Hansen (1966) [Harlow's reference] has shown that real mothers impart greater security to their infants than do artificial ones. It follows, then, that there are other influential variables. Whether these other variables in the natural environment have additive or inter-active effects on attachment of the infant remains to be demonstrated. It is not surprising that other influences are present, for behavior may always have multi-ple causes.

Breast. When in an ancillary study we held the relatively more powerful variable of contact comfort constant while offering two mothers, one with a lactating breast and the other without, monkey babies showed a clear preference for a mother with a breast. There is little doubt that the act of feeding with accom-panied nuzzling adds to the bond of infant to mother (Harlow & Zimmermann, 1959).

Rocking. In the same Harlow–Zimmermann study (1959), we found that monkey babies preferred a rocking cloth mother to one that did not rock. That preference persisted for most of a year, as did the preference for a lactating mother over one not lactating; at one year of age, these two variables had lost most of their force. The preference for rocking is similar to that in human babies, but in the case of these monkeys we were able to demonstrate that the monkey baby has a stronger affectional tie to a mother who rocks than to one who does not.

Warmth. Studies to follow up the foregoing were carried out to determine the relative power of warmth as a mother variable. For the first 20 days of life, warmth was more influential than surface contact in controlling the baby mon-keys' responses; after that, surface contact became more important.

How many other variables may be influential in infant attachment to mother is an empirical question. However, Bowlby (1969) has offered a theory of infant bonding or attachment based on an infant's instincts, which he said are species-linked and which appear variously as to time and conditions in the baby's first year.

Bowlby has argued that three such instinctual mechanisms keep an infant in contact with a mother. They are suckling, clinging, and following. These and re-lated mechanisms are all part of a single affectional device. Bowlby's theory adds rich possibilities for accommodating our data and others', perhaps without contradiction within the realm of primate behavior. An example of evidence for the innateness of suckling is shown by the work of Kessen and Mandler (1961 [Harlow's reference]), where neonates not yet fed by breast or bottle were both quieted and prevented from upset by suckling on a pacifier.

Consequences of Deprivation
from Contact Comfort

The relative importance of contact comfort, even contact from an inanimate object, is shown by a comparison of babies with and without contact with a soft mother. In one of our studies as yet unpublished, our monkey babies, separated at birth from their real mothers and having no more than a bare wire mother, failed to develop affectional responses to her.

When these babies deprived of contact comfort were placed in a room bare of objects except for wire and cloth-covered mothers and a wooden toy cricket the size of the infant, these baby monkeys cowered in a corner, buried their heads, and rocked back and forth. They neither responded to the cloth mother nor showed any interest in her, but they were clearly afraid of the cricket.

By contrast, monkey babies reared on the cloth mother at first ran to her while looking fearfully at the cricket. Then they gradually relaxed, slowly slid away from the mother, and in a short time were playing with the toy cricket.

CHAPTER
7

Writing with Style

Take a reader's perspective. Egocentric writing is self-defeating; you cannot reach an audience without thinking about that audience. Too much research writing was not written *for* anyone, only *by* someone. How can you focus on readers? Adopt a writing style that takes into account your readers' ability to understand.

ORGANIZING RESEARCH REPORTS

1. Research reports should begin immediately with a problem. Begin with the concept that will give readers the most encompassing idea.

2. Do not hold information back in the belief that readers will need background first.

3. Begin with language that is revealing. Adopt the position of giving away information as though there is limited space to write and little time.

4. Open with sentences that show intensity, like the following openings to fictitious articles:

   This was a survey of physicians to determine if they . . .

   In this study I have shown that Trapp's (1991) theory . . .

   I was looking in this study for correlations among 17 variables related to success in business. My intention was to demonstrate the presence of three factors . . .

   This study was designed to reveal what proportion of mechanical engineers offer the same solution to the . . . problem. I reasoned that . . .

   Three hours every day for five months, two observers watched children to identify their strategies for solving problems. We hypothesized that any time . . .

Direct order of presentation was expressed forcefully in an editorial in the *San Francisco Chronicle* (December 19, 1981) entitled "Burger on Prison Reform":

Chief Justice Warren Burger put his message on prison reform across by means of a simple straightfoward question. "Are we going to build more 'warehouses,'" he asked, "or should we change our thinking and build factories with fences around them where we will first train inmates and then have them engage in useful production?"

That can often be the best way to make a necessary point. Not slip into it obliquely with subtle shadings. But posit the question baldly. The answer then becomes obvious.*

Now picture a timed comprehensive examination for a doctoral degree. Several students are concentrating on the same question. Naturally, all are anxious to give answers that impress and satisfy professors. Follow two of the examinees. Ask yourself how Student I and Student II differ in their first few sentences. What differs after that?

*© *San Francisco Chronicle.* Reprinted by permission.

Student I reads the question quickly to conserve time, begins writing just as quickly, takes ideas as they appear, and maintains a fast pace; accomplishes a lengthy answer with thorough coverage. Time runs out.

Student II reads the question carefully to get the gist of the question, reflects to be confident of the central issue, writes first to expose the central issue, and takes ideas in the order of their relevance to the central issue. Time runs out.

Now, who has the most convincing answer? The winner, hands down, is Student II. Remember that professors know just what they want in an answer—and a rambling discourse is not what professors want. The most persuasive response is one that comes out obviously and quickly. Now, suppose both students' papers contain a response to the heart of the question. In the first, it is two-thirds of the way through; in the second, it is in the first sentence and immediately following. Are the answers equally worthy? Of course not. A reader can't tell how Student I judged the importance of various elements in the question. Student I, who has written by free association, is likely to have emphasized whatever coincidental ideas happened to come up.

If you are a busy professor giving the examination, you will want to know, in the shortest reading time, whether a student can sense the main element of the question and give a direct and relevant answer. If a student does not expose the main element first, how will a professor know that the student can distinguish central concepts from minor ones?

Say First What Readers Want to Know

You approach a stranger in a city and ask directions to the Belvedere Hotel. "Hello," you say. "Can you direct me to . . . ?"

"Oh, I'm glad you asked," says the warm, responsive city dweller. "Tropolis is a marvelous city! You should see our opera house and theaters. Oh, have you had the harbor cruise?"

"Yes," you say in haste.

"Well now, to the Belvedere. If you go straight down this street, you'll see Fairmont Park—it has a fine aviary, and don't miss the flowers—this is peak blooming season. Now, next . . ."

You interrupt, "But my husband has been waiting at the Belvedere since 5:00."

You see the point: Say what your readers or listeners want, and say it *first*. Take this as a superordinate principle: In expository writing, give information in direct order of importance. Give the most central concept first. Don't creep up on it; don't build background for it; don't dally to avoid the impression of abruptness. Be abrupt—that is, direct. Success in writing journal copy, a thesis, or a dissertation means a reader will know all that is important to know in the shortest possible time.

Minor concepts and preliminaries don't organize thinking. In following an escalating text from minor to more important ideas, readers of research and readers of a mystery will be puzzled as they read, but they will not get the same satisfaction. Readers in each case will raise certain hypotheses about their reading, come to doubt those hypotheses, then make up new ones. Either reader (research or mystery) will say subvocally, "I know what this is about (who did it);

it is about JKLM (the butler)." Then, further along, "No, it is about MNOP (the maid)." Is anything lost in this process? For a reader of research, two valued commodities are lost: (a) time, which is lost in searching back and forth for cues identifying a research purpose, and (b) memory for details that have weak links to each other. Readers of mysteries enjoy sensing first one purpose, then another. Readers of escalating research reports do not.

Comprehension and memory benefit from their link to a central concept. A central concept is one that has the greatest organizing power to give a reader the most encompassing grasp of what follows. Van Dijk and Kintsch (1983) have referred to *macropropositions* as propositions with global meaning derived from other propositions set out in sentences. According to them, macropropositions control the processing of local information. The earlier a macroproposition is understood, the better.

The order between and within sections is important.   Research theses, by tradition, are written in a sequence: problem, method, results, discussion. This usual order between sections of research reports is generally acknowledged and generally practiced. If you stop to think about it, you can see why that customary sequence is helpful to readers. Each successive element builds on the last and makes it easier for readers to take the next step.

How to Write Headings

1. Use enough headings. Most writers use too few.
2. Headings reveal organization. Look at the order of your headings and correctly subordinate them (see your style manual).
3. Write headings that anticipate and give away information that follows them.
4. Consider the power of a heading to communicate. Make them bring out the main concept in the passage to follow.
5. Write headings that are long enough to be understood. Though not always necessary, it is not wrong to write a heading that is two or three lines long. Judge headings by their success in reaching readers with the right information.

Headings should be long enough.   Headings are valued much more for the information they contain than for their brevity. Although headings are limited by length, they should never be so short that they fail to convey the information intended. Include prepositions, verbs, and articles. Test your headings by asking someone, "What does this mean?

Compose headings that anticipate correctly.   Write headings that *reveal the central point* of a passage or section. That makes it possible to scan the headings and get the gist of an article. A main heading like "Method," though only a single word, is satisfactory because it anticipates many equally important subheadings, all of which are methods. The more specialized or nonstandard the information, the longer a heading must be.

Think about the differences in content of three passages covered by the following three headings:

"Montessori's Theory"
"Montessori's Hypothesis That . . ."
"The Benefits of Montessori's Theory for . . ."

In the first instance, readers will expect a general exposition of Montessori's theory. The second heading will express a hypothesis. Why? Montessori had numerous hypotheses; this heading tells which one, and the text is an exposition of ideas about that hypothesis. The third heading properly anticipates a list of benefits for a limited theory. Now suppose you shorten the last heading to "Benefits." The shortened heading puts an increased burden on the text immediately preceding it to give the information the heading itself should carry.

I recently heard a renowned young scholar and journal editor talking about his view of human intelligence as consisting of various forms of adaptiveness. As one argument, he said that the best known psychologists are not distinguished from the less well known by the brilliance of their research plans or the sophistication of their data analyses. They differ, he said, in the way they report their work. Recognized scholars know how to highlight the essence of their findings and bring out the arguments and evidences they wish to emphasize. In your own research papers, don't underestimate the power of headings for emphasizing your main ideas.

Headings are organizers.   A main heading, given first, is a superordinate concept, to be followed by subheadings, which are subordinate concepts. Write these headings with great care and revise them to reflect improved organization and thought.

The suggestions that follow tell how to compose headings and titles. The organization by headings is treated only briefly because organization with headings is treated thoroughly in style manuals like the *Publication Manual of the American Psychological Association* (1983). That manual recommends the use of one to five levels of headings and makes the point that all information of the same relative importance will be placed under the same level of heading throughout a paper (pp. 65–66).

The five levels adapted from the *APA Publication Manual* are:

1.   CENTERED UPPERCASE HEADING
2.   Centered Uppercase and Lowercase Heading
3.   Centered, Underlined, Uppercase and Lowercase Heading

4. Flush Left, Underlined, Uppercase
   and Lowercase Side Heading
5.   Indented, underlined, lowercase paragraph heading ending with a period. Text continues from the heading.

The only departure from the *APA Publication Manual* to be recommended here is a minor change at level 4. When level 4 headings are long, limit the width of the heading to half a page, more or less, as in the illustration. Two or three lines of heading at the left margin having approximately equal length help to distinguish level 4 from level 3 headings.

How to Write Titles

---

1. Base composition on key words representing variables and theories.

2. Avoid noncontributing and repetitive words. Don't write "A study of" or "Results from."

3. Never abbreviate.

4. Study your titles for correct emphasis and correct modifying relations.

5. Get all the essentials into a title so that it correctly anticipates content.

Use key words in a title. Titles, like headings, are valuable for the kind of information they convey. Put the main idea of a study in its title by using key words that name variables and theories. Aim for a title of about 12 words, plus or minus 3. Here are some sample titles:

Predictions from Medring Theory of Reading Speed
at Progressive Levels of Comprehension

Bankers' Decisions for Long-Term Capital
Investment in Hong Kong

Choose word order carefully. The meaning of titles and headings is very sensitive to word order. Notice what happens if you change the order: "Banker's Decisions in Hong Kong for Long-Term . . ." The *decisions* were not made in Hong Kong, the *investments* were. Now try "Bankers' Long-Term Decisions for . . ." Again, the altered word order conveys the wrong meaning. Long-term *investments,* not *decisions,* is the correct meaning.

CREATING TEXT

When composing:

1. Write most sentences with a natural word order: subject, verb (and sometimes a complement).

2. Vary the style to include compound and complex sentences.

3. Make sentences average about 20 words.

4. Write longer sentences occasionally, but make them clear.
Keep subject and verb closely associated.
Keep modifiers associated with the terms they modify.

5. Make sentences flow from one to the next; this is called coherence. It means giving your thoughts in smooth successive transitions. Don't jump large conceptual distances between sentences.
Use a heading when you change topics.

6. Keep expressions parallel; finish sentences the way you begin them—for example: "It can be learned *by* repetition, *by* emphasizing the principle, and *by* relearning."

7. Use ordinary language; favor common words and expressions. Avoid catch phrases and jargon. Even well-established jargon should be used sparingly.

Create Most Sentences with a Natural
Word Order

The easiest sentences to read and understand are short and simple in structure, and follow a natural word order: subject, verb, complement. Ideally, the *subject* will be the first possible word. A *verb* will follow the subject and, with it, make a statement. A *complement* is a noun that follows reasonably from the subject–verb relationship, although not all sentences have a complement.

Make Most Sentences Short

Write sentences that average about 20 words, allowing a few long sentences that are understandable and efficient. Keep the vocabulary simple; in particular, minimize the number and length of noun compounds (for example, *metal cabinet hardware,* a three-word compound). Long sentences that express too many thoughts are hard on readers. The following complex sentence is too long:

> Again, on the topic of interest to memory theorists and educators, an interpretation to be made in schema theory is that the mental representations that develop during perception and comprehension, and elaborate through these processes, are not divisible as parts with simple functions, but must be understood as a totality.

Separating the ideas into several sentences, we have:

> Again, on the topic of interest to memory theorists and educators, there are mental representations. According to schema theory, mental representations arise and elaborate from perception and comprehension. Moreover, in such theory, mental representations are totalities that cannot be understood as simple functions based on their individual parts. Although mental representations from perception and comprehension are often analyzed separately, they can be understood only as a totality.

Make Your Exposition Flow
from One Sentence to the Next

Flow of discourse is called *coherence.* When sentences cohere within and without, the progress of ideas is successive and logical. All the logic must be on paper, however, not just in your mind. *Disconnection* describes the problem of small, unrelated islands of ideas. The first of the two following paragraphs lacks coherence, but the second includes connectives (italicized) to make the ideas cohere:

> Paragraphs are a series of related sentences. The thesis statement, or topic sentence, reveals a writer's purpose. Topic sentences, like other sentences, should be complete and grammatical. They should also summarize a paragraph and reveal what kind of evidence is required to support the thesis.

> Paragraphs are a series of sentences related to each other through a topic sentence, a sentence containing the general thesis of the paragraph. *Moreover,* a topic sentence is a concise expression of a writer's purpose. *Even more than a summary,* a topic sentence may hint at what sequence of ideas should follow and what kind of evidence will support it.

Local cohesion is the joining of ideas from sentence to sentence. The fore-going paragraph illustrates what is called local cohesion, or cohesion between phrases and sentences. Important devices to get local cohesion are (a) the deliberate inclusion of important details, and (b) the use of *coordinating conjunctions* and *subordinating conjunctions.* Test the coherence of your paragraphs by identifying the topic sentence to see if it is broad enough to cover what you have written and to see if you have omitted essential details.

Conjunctions are connectives that relate one sentence to another or join the ideas of one paragraph to another. Examples of words that connect are *moreover, therefore, so, yet, nevertheless,* and *also.* Sometimes several words together make good connectives, as in the foregoing example: *even more than a summary; that, of course, means;* and *going a bit farther.* Conjunctions are important devices for gaining local coherence—that is, coherence from sentence to sentence. Here are some useful conjunctions and conjunctive adverbs:

To cap an argument	*To limit a point*	*To accept a point*
further	in particular	granted
or furthermore	especially	no doubt
hence	generally	honestly
in short	frequently	of course
on the whole	normally	nevertheless
thus	occasionally	but then
consequently	then again	

Some adjectives and pronouns are good general connectives: *this, that, these, those.* In using, them, however, make sure the referent is clear from the previous sentence. It often helps to say *this problem,* or *this theory.* Words emphasizing quantity sometimes connect sentences: *many, few, every one, several, not any,* and *most.*

Subordinating conjunctions connect ideas by weakening or modifying a relation. A subordinating conjunction gives limited rank to a clause it introduces, as in, ''A is true *unless* B'' or ''I can solve the problem *unless* one of the terms is missing'' or ''You had better start writing *lest* time run out.'' There is some danger of the overuse of subordinating conjunctions. Strunk and White (1979) advised emphasizing nouns and verbs to make writing forceful. Don't over-modify.

Global cohesion means joining ideas to a central purpose. Global cohesion is a writing strategy for presenting a big picture. You can get global cohesion by arranging paragraphs so they make a progressive argument or so that they progressively expose or teach. All of these paragraphs, taken together, are required to support a major proposition—what van Dijk and Kintsch (1983) called a *macroproposition.* A succession of paragraphs supports a macroproposition the way the sentences of a paragraph support its topic sentence. As with local cohesion, global cohesion gives easy flow of ideas.

To get global cohesion, you need a master plan like one that should be in an introduction to a research report. If, in an introduction, you first have an explanatory expression of a research problem, including suppositions and their bases (presuppositions), and an operational expression of a problem, then the introduction should have global cohesion, provided each of these parts does its job. There is an overall logic that joins them in a succession of ideas that fit together and make the whole understandable to readers.

Keep Expressions Parallel

Parallel expression means consistent form. A serial list is easy to follow when the items are parallel. For example, there is a serial list of seven imperatives in the box at the beginning this section, headed "Creating Text." Those imperatives have a rhythm or consistent form. Just as a serial list should be parallel, so should a series of headings be parallel when they are at the same level and have a similar purpose.

Notice the change of form in this awkward sentence: "Problems in the cities include (a) homeless people, (b) drugs have created a crisis, and (c) the unemployed are on welfare." Made parallel, the sentence reads: "Among problems of city people are homelessness, addiction, unemployment, and entrapment in welfare."

This next sentence is not parallel because of a switch away from a participle: "The teacher not only was teaching [participle] but tutored the students as well." This is better written as: "She not only was teaching [participle], but tutoring [participle] as well."

Choose Appropriate Words

Use terms consistently throughout your report.   Don't confuse readers by introducing any variation in terms. Resist the idea that changing terms is the way to give your writing variety. Readers coming upon a new term will not know if you intend a different meaning.

Use an appositive to define an unfamiliar word.   Sometimes you must use unfamiliar words because they have a precise meaning for a certain topic. When you do, provide a definition. This is easily done with an *appositive,* a definition placed after an unfamiliar word within the same sentence—for example, "*hermeneutics,* 'the interpretation of texts,' has come also to mean 'the interpretation of social actions.'" Another example: "It was nothing but *fortuity,* a purely chance event."

Use ordinary words.   Select the simplest and most obvious words that mean what you intend. Vocabulary and length will interact to govern how readable a sentence is. Some people use simple vocabulary for most tasks but shift to an academic form of expression when they write. The language of research reports should not be too specialized or pretentious. For students and scientists alike, technical jargon is hard to understand. According to McCrimmon (1976), there are three chief characteristics of jargon:

1. Highly abstract diction, often technical, with a fondness for "learned" rather than "popular" words: *have the capability of* for *can, facilitate* for *make easy, implementation of theoretical decisions* for *putting a theory to use, maximize productivity* for *increase production,* and *utilization of mechanical equipment* for *use of machinery.*

2. Excessive use of the passive voice: If machines break down, they *are found to be functionally impaired*. . . . If more than half the students in a class did not make an outline before writing an essay, *It was discovered that on the part of the majority of the class population the writing of the essay was not preceded by the construction of an outline.*

3. Conspicuous wordiness, as illustrated in the examples given above. (McCrimmon, 1976, pp. 160–161)

Some people think using technical terms makes a writer sound well educated. A writer who prefers an elaborate expression like *lowered economic life opportunities* to a simple word like *poverty* may believe the long expression has the ring of sophistication. But it just sounds naive. Vanserg (1952) offered a satirical defense of jargon:

> Good Geologese has the essential merit that it not only baffles non-geologists but offers strenuous mental exercise to geologists themselves; comprehending it and translating it successfully is an intellectual triumph. The reward that it offers is second only to the satisfaction of making an original scientific discovery; in fact some scholars greatly prefer it. After all, what golfer would enjoy playing a course that had no hills or hazards? The successful writer of Geologese must provide adequate bunkers, dog-legs and sandtraps. (pp. 220–223)

Avoid jargon from education, government, and industry. Flowery jargon offends intelligent readers, who easily see its emptiness. Writers who put thought and rigor into their writing have substance behind their words. They don't need to use worn out and abstract language. The phrase *cadre of experts* gets the response: "Sure, impotents who wouldn't know the task from its solution." Similarly, institutional jargon like *programs of excellence* only evokes smiles. Here are more examples from the vast storehouse:

meeting the needs	A trite, vague expression
at-risk group	Belongs in medicine, but is becoming a catch phrase for social reformers.
viable options	Living options? A strange metaphor!
mandate	A word meant to lend importance to someone's motive or initiative
challenge	Usually, a mystifying task without a solution
critical problems	Usually, exaggerated problems with abstract solutions
crucial decisions	Another overblown adjective

Use temperate words, and don't exaggerate. Hardly anyone has ordinary problems or makes ordinary decisions anymore. They have all become critical, crucial, or vital. Have you noticed the disappearance of the word *effect* from our language? It has been replaced by *impact*. Students no longer ask, "What effect will your decision have on your committee?" They now ask, "What impact?" The word *impact* means a collision, a violent event. Don't exaggerate; use *impact* only when the effect is truly profound.

Don't create neologisms.   Usually a satisfactory word exists, making creation of a neologism or new word unnecessary. Don't tack *-ize* onto nouns or adjectives to create new words. Sophomores do that; graduate students shouldn't. The ending *-ize* means "to make or become," as in legitimate words like *crystallize, legalize,* and *civilize. Prioritize,* then, should mean to make a priority of something. But those who use *prioritize* usually mean something else: "to create a list in order of priority."

The ending *-wise,* tacked onto nouns, is equally bad, as in "The treatment was successful, score-wise," or "The computer is a useful tool, time-wise." Say instead: "The treatment was successful; scores in the experimental group were higher than those in the control group," and, "Computers save a lot of time."

In industry, the proliferation of verbs from nouns and nouns from verbs is creating a whole new language—a bad one. Skip lightly over these; you don't want to remember them:

> That is what he was *tasked* to do.
>
> *Optimize* the connection; *interface* this with that.
>
> If it's *doable,* who is to do it?
>
> When we *leverage* this component to the front, we get twice the output.

Choose words for precision of meaning.   Use specific words. It is better to say, "Five *red* index cards" and "95 *white* index cards" than "Five *colored* [general]" and "95 *plain* index cards." Similarly, avoid substituting words like *many* or *several* for numbers. "After examining *several* personality inventories" is less effective than "After examining *twelve* personality inventories."

Use concrete words: Say, "The child kicked the Bobo doll, threw toys across the playroom, and hit another child," rather than, "The child was aggressive."

Words Often Used Incorrectly

Examine the following pairs of words with different meanings; writers sometimes pick the wrong word:

> *Methodology* is the study of methods. The term *methodology* is often misused. Surgery, cabinetmaking, measurement theory, and statistical theory are all properly *methodological.* It is correct to say: "In medicine there is well-developed *methodology* for diagnosing disease; there are many methods, and these methods constitute a subject matter to be studied." It is wrong to say, "His *methodology* was to examine a blood sample." One should not refer to *a* method as methodology. It is always wrong to say, "The methodology for my study is in Chapter 2."

> *Method* is a particular, actual method, a singular case of method. Research reports have a *method* section, not to be called "methodology." It is correct to say," I used a case study *method.*"

> *Feel* is an abstraction from the sensation of touch; *feel,* then, means emotional response. You can *feel* anger or disgust, but you cannot *feel* that a theory is correct. "I *feel* ill" or "I feel great sympathy for her" are proper uses. Reserve *feel* for expressing emotion; never use it to mean judgment or belief.

Believe is a cognitive response: "I *believe* that theory is correct." The headline *Arson Felt Responsible for $100,000 Blaze* could have been written *Fire Captain Believes* . . . Say, "I *think* Margaret is correct," never, "I *feel* Margaret is correct," unless you specifically want to exclude judgment and show emotion.

Amount is used for a measured or continuous quantity: "A large amount of milk was needed for the seven children." Don't use amount with objects that are counted. Do *not* say, "Each was given an equal *amount* of marbles."

Number is used to refer to countable objects: "Each subject was given an equal *number* of marbles."

Less is used to refer to degree or quantity in a continuous variable: "Subjects appeared to be *less* disoriented during the second phase of the experiment than during the first." "Mary ate *less* than John."

Fewer is used only with countable objects and refers to number: "Children in the control group earned *fewer* [not *less*] points than children in the treatment group." "There are *fewer* errors in this paper." "Mary ate *fewer* cherries than John."

Most is used when referring to a measured or continuous quantity, not composed of individual numbers: "Julie spent *most* of her free time playing tennis." "*Most* of the medicine was taken."

Majority is used only to refer to countable, individual items. *Majority* is in contrast with *minority:* "The *majority* of participants elected Jim to preside over the meeting." "The *majority* of survey respondents were young." Don't say, "John spent the *majority* of his free time playing tennis."

Affect as a verb means "to influence," as in, "I hypothesized that alcohol consumption *affects* motor ability." As a noun, *affect* refers to feeling: "The patient showed inappropriate *affect.*"

Effect as a verb means "to bring about": "He was able to *effect* a truce between the two countries." As a noun, *effect* means "result": "We investigated the *effect* of organization on recall of prose passages."

Among is used with more than two objects: "The mother divided the candy *among* the four children." In reporting data analysis for several conditions, write, "A variance estimate *among* means was computed" (if there are more than two means).

Between is used with two objects: "The child chose *between* two toys."

Singular and Plural Words Often Misused

Singular	Plural
phenomenon	phenomena
criterion	criteria
datum	data
colloquium	colloquia
equilibrium	equilibria
index	indices *or* indexes
alumnus	alumni
bacillus	bacilli

Singular	*Plural*
homeostasis	homeostases
analysis	analyses
apparatus	apparatuses
appendix	appendices *or* appendixes
crisis	crises
sequela	sequelae

Note that *sequela* is parallel to *sequel* but is in common use only in medicine; in other realms of discourse, use *sequel* as the singular form.

Fill Your Ideas Out Completely

Don't compress explanations.   Readers need full explanation so they don't have to infer meaning from skeletal expressions. Remember, readers don't know your motivations or the details of your investigation. To be a good writer, you must develop an alertness for the elements you need to make complete concepts. If your style is cryptic (compressed and heavy), you must persevere in search of a style that is complete. Like other complex habits, fullness of expression requires time.

You can compress both within and between sentences. Within sentences, compression can result from missing prepositions. Since prepositional phrases are explanatory, when you remove the prepositions, the explanation becomes a mere label. That label, lacking prepositions, is often a heavy noun–adjective string. The problem of noun–adjective strings is so vexing and so common that it is treated at length in a later section, entitled "Explain; Don't Simply Label."

Ask someone to read your writing who knows the subject matter and who will respond objectively. Quiz this reader to see if he or she has received complete ideas from your text. (Remember, your friends may hesitate to give an unfavorable judgment and may not be practiced critics.) Then study your own writing, asking, "Have I said everything essential?" Get accustomed to asking that question regularly.

In the following compressed statement of a research problem, much has been left for readers to fill in, far more than any reader can infer. In the restatement following, the necessary information has been supplied to give readers a grasp of the problem.

A compressed statement of a research problem	I propose to study reading as subvocalizing nonsense words, either pronounceable or unpronounceable. My purpose is to determine if unpronounceable syllables (non-English) will be recognized with greater latency than pronounceable syllables. I hypothesize that phonemic coding is needed to search an internal lexicon.
A better statement of a research problem. Here fewer inferences are required	I propose to investigate the necessity for a reader to re-code a word from graphic to phonemic form before that reader can recognize the word as belonging to his lexicon. I believe that recoding is necessary for recognition. To test my supposition, I plan to measure subvocalizations from electromyographic tracings taken from a

reader's tongue as that reader attempts to read both pronounceable (English) and unpronounceable (nonsense) syllables. If a phonemic response is needed before a word can be recognized, a reader will recognize a pronounceable syllable more quickly than an unpronounceable one. Vocalization latencies are shorter for pronounceable words if my supposition is correct.

Keep Values Out

Don't editorialize.   Objectivity is essential in research writing. Be factual; don't interject comments that are judgmental or opinionated. Opinionated commet is illustrated in the following: "Smith and Dodge (1991) have recently contributed a *well-conceived* and *well-executed* study."

Don't overjustify your research.   Some forms of valuing comment are worse than others because of the particular words used. Words that overstate a case or make preposterous claims obviously damage a writer's credibility. Inexperienced writers sometimes start their papers with justifications of a topic—bad practice in itself, but made substantially worse by the use of certain words:

In this study I examined the *critical* question of . . .

This was an investigation of a *practical* application of theory to the *important* problem of . . .

This study was designed to examine the *crucial* problem . . .

Inclusion of variables *vital* to the investigation of . . .

Then, too, there are instances when young investigators apologize for research that does not generalize readily to real life. Statements telling the potential application of research are not necessary, are often exaggerated, and give the impression of naiveté. Debate over the value of a research effort should occur before it begins, not in reporting what was done. Research embodies its own justification. It is never necessary to apologize for it, because intelligent readers can see if and how research applies to theory or is useful. Describe your research clearly, with factual statements, and let readers form their own idea of the value of the work.

When You Modify, Take Careful Aim

1. Choose modifiers to fit your intention. Don't modify what you don't have to.
2. Place adjectives next to the nouns they modify—more often than not in front of a noun.
3. Place adverbs next to the verbs they modify.
4. Use participles sparingly, and give them a correct subject. Using participles in research writing is risky, but they do add variety to your text. Avoid dangling participles. For example, "*Dusting* the sample, there appeared a strange symbol on its surface," should be "*Dusting* the sample, she discovered a strange symbol on its surface."

Don't overuse modifiers; when you use them, attach them where they belong. Strunk and White (1979, p. 71) advised writers to use mainly nouns and verbs. Adjectives and adverbs, they said, can't usually salvage weak or inaccurate nouns and verbs. Their admonition emphasizes the clear, strong effect of words without modifiers. Use modifiers only when they are needed for emphasis or to clarify the correct meaning of a noun or verb. Consider the following:

> Children sulk.
> Young children sulk.
> Young children sulk until they learn sulking is maladaptive.

Although *children sulk* has a crispness that the other expressions lack, each statement has a place demanded by its meaning. As a generalization, *children sulk* works well unless the generalization must be limited. Don't use modifiers to set limits that are unnecessary for your purpose. If a study has nothing to do with sex, don't use sex as a modifier; for example, "Not all children sulk, although the severity varies with sex."

Don't misapply modifiers in research reports. It is easy to put a modifier in the wrong place. Place modifiers physically close to the word or words they should modify. Misapplied modifiers are often the result of compression, the incomplete filling out of an idea.

Wrong:	Subjects were to recall a series of words presented to the left ear or a series to the right *ear by earphones.*
Right:	Subjects were to recall either a series of words *presented by earphone* to the left ear or a different series *presented by earphone* to the right ear.

Wrong:	The chemist walked from the laboratory *holding the flask.*
Right:	The chemist, *holding the flask,* walked from the laboratory.

SAYING WHAT YOU INTEND

Explain; Don't Simply Label

Institutional language often includes peculiar labels and local jargon, usually in the form of noun–adjective strings and long noun compounds. Ann Landers, in a 1977 column, reported the complaint of a parent who could not understand a message received from the principal of his child's school. Here is that message:

> Our school's *cross-graded, multi-ethnic, individualized learning program* is designed to enhance the concept of an *openended learning program* with emphasis on a continuum of *multi-ethnic, academically enriched learning,* using the *identified intellectually gifted child* as the agent or director of his own learning. Major emphasis is on *cross-graded, multi-ethnic learning* with the main objective being to learn respect for the uniqueness of a person [italics added to identify labeling word strings].

The parent wrote back:

I have a college degree, speak two foreign languages and know four Indian dialects. I've attended a number of county fairs and three goat ropings but I haven't the faintest idea as to what the hell you are talking about. (*Phoenix Gazette,* September 14, 1977)

Writers who get caught up in institutional language offend thoughtful readers who abhor gibberish. You can either toss a label at your readers, or take the trouble to explain the concept. The practice of labeling in lieu of explaining is widespread, and many writers have no idea that they are labeling what they should explain. Some of the most egregious instances of the use of word strings that only label a concept occur in reports of research.

Well-known labels communicate; spontaneously created ones don't. When a label does what it was intended to do, a reader instantly recognizes it and understands its meaning. Analyze the compound *secretary-treasurer;* it is satisfactory because we all know it. *Secretary-treasurer* evokes an image of a person whose secretarial and treasurer responsibilities are a composite, where neither term is subordinate.

For an experienced adult, *lamp post* is a satisfactory label. However, *lamp post* differs from *secretary-treasurer* in that *lamp* and *post* are not symmetrical to each other; one cannot so easily say *post lamp.* When young children first encounter the term, the words *lamp* and *post* can function together as a single concept only if children correctly interpret the relation of lamp to post. Don't count on it. Although young children may know both terms as separate concepts, they are not likely to know their combined meaning (with the emphasis given to *post*).

Penelope Keith, in "Spider's Web," a television adaptation of Agatha Christie's play, showed how the inversion of two terms changes meaning: "A horse chestnut" she said, "or a chestnut horse— . . . [it] makes all the difference" (Christie, 1956, p. 74).

An adult is no better off than a child if that adult knows only individual terms in a compound but does not know the nominal meaning of the complete label. Common noun compounds like *lamp post* and *card catalogue* present no difficulties for adult readers, but that is not true for words joined spontaneously into compounds without explanatory connectives between them. Unfamiliar labels slow readers down as they guess at a meaning.

Labels compress meaning and make writing heavy. The following sentences illustrate the heaviness that comes from using too many labels:

Investigators of the *classical retroactive interference paradigm* have asked subjects to read an *original biographical paragraph* with *specified references* from the *original paragraph.* Following the *experimental interpolated biographical paragraph* they have typically given a *multiquestion cued recall test* to measure recall from the *original biographical paragraph.* (46 words, with labeling strings italicized)

Reducing the labels to explanation and attempting to make all the essential points in this difficult passage, we end up with 52 words that are easier to read:

> Typically, investigators of *retroactive interference* have asked subjects to read a paragraph of biography, then read another paragraph of biography, constructed experimentally to interfere with memory for the first. After reading the *second paragraph,* the subject has taken a test having cues to prompt his memory for elements in the *first paragraph.*

The first labeling string has two superfluous words, *classical* and *paradigm,* probably designed to sound technical and sophisticated. Both words are pretentious; in the revised paragraph, *typical* has replaced classical to tell readers that the method is ordinary in these studies of forgetting. *Paradigm,* an unjustified claim that the method is universal or is a model, has been dropped.

Retroactive interference has been retained as a label in the revised paragraph because it is a common expression in studies of memory and forgetting. Nevertheless, because neophytes also read research, the revised paragraph contains a description of retroactive interference, so that undergraduates and other readers can make a start toward understanding it.

Observe, next, how *original biographical paragraph* has become *a paragraph of biography.* The easiest way to break up nominal strings is to write prepositions. *Of biography* is intrinsically clear and free of the ambiguity that often accompanies the *-al* suffixes. *Biography* should be emphasized, not *paragraph.* Therefore, *biogaphy* should not have been written as an adjective (*biographical*).

Replace Labels with Explanations:

1. *Study a sizable sample of your writing.* Find out if you use frequent strings of nouns and adjectives unrelieved by prepositions and verbs.

2. *Use prepositions and verbs to break up word strings.* When these words are added, the word order may change to give a correct emphasis and make modifying relations more obvious.

3. *Minimize the length of word strings.* Long word strings increase the possibility of unintentional interword associations. For example, the expression in medical technology *leur lock tip syringe* is better written with a preposition: "She held a syringe *with* a leur locking tip."

4. *Be careful with word order, especially in headings and titles.* If you write *aesthetic research,* for example, the meaning can be either "research with aesthetic qualities" or "research on aesthetic topics."

5. *Purge superfluous words.* Some of the worst noun–adjective strings include null words, words that make no contribution to meaning. Notice the null effect of the italicized word in the following: "mechanical engineering *area* focus." Change the word order, and drop *area:* Now you have *focus on mechanical engineering.* Another common superfluous term is *situation,* as in "a classroom *situation*" or "a fourth-down *situation.*" Omit it.

6. *Avoid unnecessary technical labels.* If your goal is to write with clarity, you should use the simplest and most explanatory expressions. If you are aiming to impress your readers, you are apt to choose word combinations that sound complex and make your text look technical.

7. *Explain uncommon labels.* If a label is necessary, explain it with an *appositive,* a definition placed next to the term in the same sentence. In the foregoing sentence, an appositive was used to define *appositive:* "a definition placed next . . ."

8. *Minimize the use of abbreviations.* Only three conditions for using abbreviations are acceptable to the Publications Board of the American Psychological Association: (a) when an abbreviation is better known than the complete form, (b) when the abbreviated use is conventional, and (c) when awkward repetitions can be avoided or space saved (see the *APA Publication Manual,* second edition, 1974, p. 33).

9. *Avoid using suffixes like -al that may give a wrong emphasis.* If you write *temperamental characteristic,* be sure you don't mean *characteristic temperament.* Don't write "*historical teacher*" for *history teacher* or *historical editor* for *history editor* (unless you really mean an editor with historical significance rather than simply an editor in the field of history).

Notice how noun–adjective strings can be changed to create exposition.
Noun–adjective strings flourish in bureaucratic language, even in universities, where fidelity of communication is a main purpose. Here are some word strings that will perplex or amuse you, but don't let the humor distract you from a realization that these verbal monstrosities can do serious damage to your writing and speaking. The substituted expressions indicate the apparent intended meanings:

Committee to Feed the Hungry President	President of the Committee to Feed the Hungry
a three-in-one shot for airborne cat diseases	for cats, a three-in-one shot against airborne diseases
disposable toddler diapers	disposable diapers for toddlers
United Rubber, Cork, Linoleum and Plastic Workers of America	United Workers in the Manufacture of Cork, Linoleum, and Plastics
Emergency Building Temperature Restrictions Certificate of Building Compliance	Certificate of Compliance with Temperature Restrictions under Building Emergencies
Multifunctional Bilingual Education Indian Agencies	This heading is a *nonfunctional lingual atrocity* (I couldn't resist trying a three-term label myself).
Moffett's four-stage speaker–subject continuum (an awkward string, though the hyphens help)	Moffett's continuum *through* four stages *from* speaker *to* subject
the huge Mayo Clinic medical library	The Mayo Clinic's huge medical library *or* The medical library of the huge Mayo Clinic (Does *huge* modify clinic or library?)
handicapped restroom	restroom for the handicapped
National Postanesthesia Nurse Awareness Week	National Awareness Week for Postanesthesia Nurses
Punishment of Death Conference	Conference on Punishment by Means of a Death Penalty

Point to the Correct Time with Verb Tense

The tense of a verb signals a past, present, or future event, or it may signal a timeless event.

1. Use past tense often because most events in research will be past.
   - This *was* [not *is*] a study to determine if . . .
   - Johnson and Smith *found that* when they . . .
   - Weber *believed* . . . [not *believes,* because we will allow Weber to change his mind].

2. Use present tense for giving a fact or principle.
   - London *is* in England.
   - People *migrate* toward ample food supplies.
   - Children *read* faster as they gain experience.

3. Use future tense (or future perfect) in proposing a study.
   - I *will use* a continuous narrative to describe.
   - An ethnographic analysis *will be used.*

4. Use present perfect tense to refer to ongoing states of mind or actions.
   - Eisner *has been arguing* that . . .
   - It *has been* Rossi's position that . . .

   Use past tense, rather than present perfect, when you refer to persons who are no longer part of the action. Don't say: Aristotle (or Dewey) *has taken* a view that . . . . Say: Aristotle *took* a view . . .

Use past tense for past events.   Past tense is appropriate to describe your own research—for example, "In the study *reported* here, the relation of mental image to recall of prose *was investigated"; "subjects answered"; "data were analyzed."*

Here, in a reference to Carl Rogers, is an idea Rogers expressed years ago: "Rogers 19--) *defines* client-centered therapy as nondirective therapy." *Wrong;* Rogers *defined* client-centered therapy in 19--. A past event should be given a historical temper so the theorist is free to change his or her definition or belief. The use of the present tense for past events creates the impression that theorists never change.

Even for more recent references, past tense should be used because time has passed. Thus, you should write, "Moore (1989) *listed* three factors." Don't write, "Moore lists three factors"; Moore may sometimes choose to list two, or nine. Don't imply that Moore has a special disposition toward three.

There are widespread influences that lead us to overuse present tense. We often hear, "The president says," when the speaker is referring to a past event and should say, "The president *said.*" In expository writing, no distinction should be considered minor, for your goal is to be perfectly clear. Readers should not have to waste any mental energy to determine logical relations that can be conveyed automatically by grammatical construction. The content of research reports demands readers' full attention even when it is well written.

Tense in the entertainment world has a different purpose from tense in research reports.   In narrating a story, present tense may be used for past events so a reader can feel the immediacy of the action: "Mary tells John the time has come"; "John senses a very real problem." Similarly, a sports announcer calls out: "*He scores!*" These special circumstances call for an audience to be a part of an action. We don't want story writers and television announcers to give up special devices to make an audience *feel* the action. But there is no need for readers of research to experience the scene of action with such immediacy.

   Use present tense for timeless referents.   Present tense should be used when there is no time reference. Generalizations and principles are timeless, as in, "Sodium chloride *is* soluble in water." Notice the temporal conditions within the following sentence: "Children ordinarily *respond* [present tense] faster than adults, but in our study there *was* [past tense] no difference." The first statement is a generalization; the second a report of a past event.

   Another example: "Jones (1986) *reported* that children *learn* to speak by listening to speech sounds of other people." *Reported* refers to a past event, but *learn* refers to a generalization from events that have occurred many times in the past; it does not refer to particular children.

   When deciding whether a certain instance should be expressed in past or present tense, determine the temporal status of that instance. If results apply to a sample of particular subjects who participated, use past tense. Write, "A child's perceived sense of humor *was correlated* with a rating by the child's classmates ($r = .69$, $p = .025$." These were real children, and the data from them were correlated.

   When your intention is to describe an entire population, use present tense. Therefore, write, "Children's perceived sense of humor *is correlated* with the way other children view their sense of humor." The inference is based on many studies, but it does not refer to particular children but, rather, to children in general.

   Theoretical generalizations have no time reference. Observe the use of present tense in the following: "According to Torricelli, the sea-of-air hypothesis *is* basis for explaining how a water pump works" (not "*was* basis" unless you are telling how views have changed). Notice that there is no reference to a past event; that is, the declaration is undated. In referring to a theoretical construct, use present tense for operations within the theory, but use present perfect or past tense to refer to the theorist, as in: "Piaget *believed* (theorized, taught, speculated) that children *do not conserve* length at age three." Piaget is dead; therefore you say, "Piaget *believed*," or use past perfect tense, "Piaget *had believed*." But the generalization *do not conserve* is undated; we say it has *perennial force*.

   Use present perfect tense to express continuing action.   Make frequent use of present perfect tense, which is used to show continuity or repetition of actions where specific time is unimportant. The present perfect tense has been neglected, to the disadvantage of writers. Use present perfect tense to refer to an ongoing event. You can say, for example, "van Dijk and Kintsch *have been emphasizing* such concepts as narrative superstructures and semantic macrostructures."

   Although the actions are past, the emphasis is on continuity. We assume these writers are still emphasizing superstructures. If you say, "Jaynes has been claiming that . . . ." it means you cannot put temporal bounds on the claim. As far as anyone knows, Jaynes's repeated claims continue to the present. Notice that present perfect tense is used to refer to *real* events that are repeating, but it is not used to express generalizations. Try using present perfect tense when you want to convey a continuous intention or action that is also current and has not lost its force.

> ***Use future tense in proposals.***   Use future tense when you propose a study for a thesis or a dissertation. A sentence like, "I *will* draw a sample of 30 children" is correct. Future tense is consistent with the time to be communicated and enables you to avoid the indirectness and tentativeness projected by the use of *would* or *should*. Don't write, "I *would* draw a sample of 30 children."

Point to Objects with the Definite Article

> The definite article, *the,* is needed to identify a previously mentioned object (*The* hat I referred to is here.) Overuse of *the,* however, destroys its value as a pointer. A solution is to avoid *the* as often as possible.
>
> 1. Use the definite article only when it is needed to point to an object already identified or when convention requires it.
> 2. Practice using an indefinite article with a noun when it is first introduced. Then in subsequent text you can use the definite article with that noun to identify the object as the one already referred to:
>   - *A* test was used to measure aptitude of my subjects for mathematics.
>   - After *the* test had been administered . . .

In English-speaking countries, indiscriminate use of *the* has all but ruined its value as a pointer. In expository writing, the definite article points to or identifies its referent. When you say, "Bring *the* dog," you don't ordinarily mean the neighbor's dog or a stray mutt. But if you say, "Bring me *a* dog," any dog will do.

The distinction isn't trivial, for in complex explanations, readers are dependent on *the* to identify the specific referent intended. By contrast, readers know that *a* or *an* signals the general case without reference to any particular object. Don't use the definite article with the general case; save it to point to a particular referent.

Shank and Abelson (1977) said that *articles link concepts within a script* and offered a brief narrative that ends: "John went to a park. He asked the midget for a mouse. He picked up the box and left" (p. 40). A reader of the entire narrative is not prepared for *the* midget or *the* box because these were not previously mentioned in the narrative. Then, said the authors, "We are incapable of connecting the last two lines of the story without a great deal of effort." The story "allows us no reference to a standard situation in which midgets, mouses, boxes and parks relate" (p. 40). *Scripts,* according to Shank and Abelson, are connected narratives; articles are connectors.

Indefinite articles designate one member of a class of nouns when that member can be any one of those members. For example, normal curves vary both in how large they are (how many cases are in them) and in how much variation there is in them (their standard deviations); some are big, some small, some tall, some short. "*A* normal curve" refers to any one of these without discriminating their particulars. To say "*the* normal curve" is misleading when no particular normal curve has been identified, for there are as many normal curves as there are normal variables.

A method to make referents clear.   When you first refer to an object, use an *in*definite article. Continue with an indefinite article until you intend a reader to know that you are referring to that same object; then use *the*.

> A lens has been mounted at the front of a light-limiting enclosure. When light passes through *the* lens . . . [or, When light passes through *that* lens . . .

If a definite article is used first, readers search for *the* object they apparently missed in a foregoing sentence. Suppose the following sentence appears on a second page without prior mention of a survey: "She administered *the* survey to a group of 30 people seated around tables."

"What survey?" readers are likely to ask. "I don't remember any mention of a survey."

Use Pronouns Unambiguously

> *It, they, he, this, that, these,* and *those,* placed at the beginning of a sentence, are hazardous. Any one of these pronouns may not have a clear referent, whether it is placed at the beginning of a sentence or further on.
>
> **1.** Make antecedents of pronouns obvious: "*This* formula is correct," not "*This* is correct."
> **2.** Repeat nouns in place of some of the pronouns.

Make certain there is only one concept to which your pronoun could refer. Use *this* and *it* infrequently, and be especially wary of starting a sentence with *either*. Repetition of nouns is prefereable to use of pronoun referents that are unclear. Notice the puzzling *it* and *this* that open the second and third sentences following:

> The theory has two forms, one which accounts for observable events and another which accounts for unobservable events. *It* may explain the predominance of certain mental acts. *This* is the primary advantage of the theory.

BEING DEFINITE AND FORCEFUL

> Take reasonable risk. Avoid weak expressions.

We teach students to use language cautiously, but we hope they will achieve balance, making neither brash assertions nor weak ones. Confident people write with directness; their styles are terse. Further, they accept a certain degree of risk in interpreting what they report. Here are two statements, one with some risk, the other soft and mushy:

> *Risky:* "No explanation is satisfactory."
>
> *Safe but empty:* "The evidences are not quite understood."

Don't overuse qualifiers. Some expressions that weaken are the following: *suggests* (the evidence *suggests*); *apparently* (it is *apparently* true); *at times; quite frequently; very* (as in *very often*); *can be* (rather than *is*).

Make Interpretations

It is your responsibility as a writer to summarize and interpret your own and others' work. That means you should tell readers how to look at evidences.

1. Extract principles or generalizations from aggregated literature. Say how and why the interpretations are justified.
2. Express the magnitudes of relations or differences. Say: "*A* is 0.41 greater than *B*," or: "These correlations are so small as to be meaningless. The r^2 of_____is only 0.06."

Do not be afraid to make interpretations. Judicious interpretation helps readers understand. But writers often overlook a reader's need for interpretation, particularly of complexities that are difficult to grasp. In reporting research, interpretations are especially needed within a rationale for a research problem, within a results section, and within a discussion; all of these should be interpretive.

Suppose you are writing a results section of a thesis and interpret as follows: "As expected, the *X* condition was much more effective than the *Y* condition." Such a sentence is forceful because you said what happened. The claim is justified if the *X* condition was much more effective *in your judgment*.

Interpret literature. The literature of a research problem should be interpreted so readers will know the status of that problem in the literature. It is not enough to list strings of citations mechanically without organizing them and putting interpretations on them. Tell your readers how these references give basis to the particular problem that you studied.

The following illustrates how interpretative language applies to an expression of a research problem:

> Of the 12 tests of the hypothesis, only 7 agree with it; moreover, the weights of the favorable evidences were small in 5 of the 7 cases. Among the favorable, Johnson (1995) has made the most complete case. In her study, _____ was .63 greater than _____. Wilson (1979) made a strong argument for [H] but only with respect to the limited aspect of _____. I must now say what justified the present investigation in view of the foregoing weak evidence for H. . . .

Observe that the language is both interpretive and to some degree bold, but it was meant to illustrate reasonable risk and qualification—hence the use of the words *only, small, strong, weak*. Notice the writer's tone in saying, "only 7." The literature attendant to a particular problem should be organized and interpreted directly to reveal an investigator's thinking about that literature. Do not make recitations in literature sections that are nothing more than a listing of somewhat related research and theory. Your credibility is strengthened when you lay out arguments both for and against your position in an evenhanded way. In principle, science writers should not use euphemisms or dodge evidences. Simple, honest, and forceful interpretations fit the task.

Use Specific Language

Favor specific words over general words.

1. Say "Concerning *store* management" rather than "Concerning the management *area*." Save *area* for geography, where it has a specific meaning.
2. Say "My *method* was ideographic" rather than "My *approach* was ideographic."

Strunk and White (1979) said to write with "definite, specific, concrete language," (p. 21), and Sheridan Baker (1976) advised, "be as concrete as you can" (p. 182). In fiction, concrete expressions permit images that make description real. In exposition, concrete language makes abstract concepts understandable.

In spite of all the praise given to the use of concrete words, abstract words are not bad words; they simply need concrete support to be understood. Some abstract words, however, either don't contribute at all or are too general. A group of such words identified by Leggett, Mead, and Charvat (1974) are called "omnibus words," meaning they have been used for too many purposes; they are vague (p. 343).

Omnibus word:	"I've been in this *field* for 30 years."
Specific word:	"I've been in *geology* for 30 years."
Omnibus word:	"I don't like this *approach*."
Specific words:	"I don't like his *slow, hesitating explanation*."

"Her *approach* in the study was regression analysis" is general and abstract. Instead, write, "Her *method* in the study was regression analysis." A specific, proper use of the word *approach* is possible, however; to say, "She approached the dog cautiously," is a specific, concrete use of the word. It has the original meaning, "to draw near."

One of the most overused words in the English language is *area*. It is an omnibus word, used indiscriminately. Don't write, "In the area of her competence." Instead, write, "Her competence is her logic." *Area* is a perfectly good geometric or geographic term; reserve it for that purpose. Write, "In the *area* where cooking takes place," or "The *area* is 15 square meters." Don't write or say, "What *area* are you studying?" Be specific; ask, "What *subject* are you studying?"

Make Minimal Use of *Would, Should,* and *Might*

Use would and should to express:

1. Ideas contrary to fact: "If respondents had marked yes, the investigator *would* have asked why."
2. As past tense of *will* and *shall:* "She explained that she *would* have analyzed all the sentences if she had been asked. She admitted she *should* have left."

Conditional sentences with words like *would, might,* and *should* are seldom needed in research reports. Avoid a tentative tone; use expressions of confidence. Suppose a graduate student has written a proposal for a thesis using the following language: "I would interpret Smith as meaning that . . . ." (Does the student really mean, "If my mentors won't criticize me for it"?) Say instead, "I have interpreted Smith to mean that . . .

Tentative: "These results *could* be interpreted as support for the hypothesis."
Confident: "These results *support* the hypothesis."
Weak: "If you *would* sign, I *would* go."
Better: "If you will sign, I will go."

Avoid Prolixity

Be brief. Don't write to impress.

Prolixity means wordiness and inefficiency in expressing an idea. Prolixity is annoying, and wordy expressions damage comprehension. *Terseness* is the opposite of prolixity; to be terse means to be concise, or even elegantly concise.

Say it modestly: avoid pedantry.   Pedantry, a serious form of prolixity, includes ostentatious displays of a large vocabulary or complex ways of expressing an idea. The word *pedantry* comes from *pedagogy* or teaching, but it emphasizes the *display* of knowledge.

Pedantic writing creeps in when an author is trying to make a good impression. Edgar Dale (1953) poked fun at the notion that writing must be pedantic to sound scholarly:

Young Alvin H. Harrison hesitatingly entered the office of Dr. Maxim S. Kleeshay and timidly inquired about his master's thesis. "What did you think of it?" he asked.

"A worthy endeavor," replied the Doctor, "but it has one major defect. It is written at too elementary a level. I would like to offer somewhat tentatively the pertinent observation that graduate students, research workers, and professors will find it too easy and effortless to read—no disciplinary value. Remember that Chancellor Hutchins once said that good education is painful. Furthermore, you haven't stated any significant challenges in your introductory paragraphs.''

''I didn't want to offer any challenges. I just wanted to make my ideas clear.''

''That's a worthy primary objective, young man. But no educational writing today should fail to point out that the world is in peril, in flux, in conflict, changing, disordered, and disunited. It's either one world or two, you know.''

''And another thing—it is interesting to note that you have a mistaken notion about communication on the scholarly level. It is obvious that you are unaware of the appropriate technical terminology in education. Your thesis is too sprightly, too simple.''

''You mean that if I am dull enough and labored enough, I'll sound scholarly?''

''A very unfortunate and inaccurate way to put it, young man. I trust that it is not inappropriate to note some examples from your own thesis and to offer some suggestions (tentative, of course) as to how these examples might be shifted into more precise and scholarly language.''

''You say on page 59, 'It will be hard to provide enough schools for the three million children entering in 1950.' It would have sounded much better if you had said, 'The phenomenon of fecundity has confronted American education with a challenge of Herculean proportions. An evaluation of the implication to the tax structure of state governments in providing adequate educational facilities is a difficult and complex task.'''

''Let me make another point. A critical analysis of your thesis discloses that you are making little use of what is called the adjectival approach in education. You speak of 'thinking.' It would be much better to refer to 'critical thinking.' Change 'an approach to the problem' to 'a constructive approach to the problem.' At one point here, you say that the teacher is given 'help in working on her problems.' I would say that she had been given 'rather definite assistance in attacking specific difficulties.' You speak of 'reading practices.' Make it 'sound reading practices.' Utilize 'basic fundamentals' and 'desirable goals' a little more. Don't use the word 'function' alone. Say 'basic function.'''

''At times I think you are too abrupt in your approach. You say, for example, that you tried Professor Blowhard's scheme of teaching reading and it did not work. You ought to use the oblique or bashful approach here and say, 'The writer does not choose to disparage the efficacy of Professor Blowhard's method of teaching reading. It is not inappropriate, however, to point out that careful scrutiny of the method shows it to be what might be called inapposite.'''

''In short, it stinks,'' replied young Harrison.

Menzel, Jones, and Boyd (1961) have written that, ''A few writers seem to feel that if the reader can understand too easily, the paper is not really 'scientific.' They regard the exposition as a kind of contest: if the reader finds nothing to puzzle him, the author loses the game'' (p. 88).

Be Brief

Short, simple statements have strong, memorable effects on readers: ''To eliminate bias, I . . . ,'' not, ''In order to eliminate the possibility of bias . . .'' Write:

"Most research on . . . ," not, "The greatest percentage of research concerning . . ."

Wordy Expression	Better Alternative
to be deficient in	to lack
the greatest percentage of	most
a majority of	most
it is clear that	clearly
it is obvious that	obviously
in the event that	if
in all cases	always, invariably
in order to	to
in the field of	in
in the area of	in
owing to the fact that	because
except for the fact that	except that
for the reason that	because
at this point in time	now
it is often the case that	often

Omit Superfluous Words

In certain expressions, some words serve no purpose at all. In the following phrases, the italicized word adds nothing:

"In a problem-solving *situation.*" Say instead: "In solving problems"

"In a hospital *setting*" and "In a classroom *setting*"

"In a free-play *activity.*" *Free play* is sufficient. Notice the difference when the word is not superfluous: "I need more *activity.*"

"Closed circuit television *system*" and "Theoretical *system*"

"Treatment *condition*" rather than simply *treatment*

"A reading *approach*" or "A listening *approach*"

"A cooperative games *program*" rather than simply *cooperative games*

"Running in a maladaptive *manner.*" Say: "Running *maladaptively.*"

Emphasize the Active Voice

> Use the active voice, but don't create a substitute actor in order to do it.

A writer must choose to write in either the active or the passive voice. Your choice will make a difference in how readable and how forceful your writing is. Although all writers should make some use of both voices, stylists show an increasing preference for the active voice. A verb is active when it expresses an *action performed by its subject:* "The boy hit the ball." A verb is passive when it expresses an *action performed upon its subject:* "The ball was hit by the boy."

Here, the passive expression emphasizes *ball* over *boy.* The active expression has more punch. Sometimes the choice of an active or passive verb is a matter of personal taste. Unless used sparingly, however, the passive voice will deaden the discourse and require readers to use more energy to follow it: "At the beginning of his senior year, a second-hand typewriter was purchased by Bill, and a course in typing was signed up for by him."

The following guidelines from the *American National Standards for the preparation of scientific papers for written or oral presentation* (1979, p. 12) concern appropriate use of active and passive voice:

1. Use active voice "when a verb concerns the interaction of inanimate objects." Thus, write "The drug acts on the membrane" rather than "The membrane is acted upon by the drug".

2. Do not use a passive construction like "It is thought" or "It is suggested" when a verb concerns your own belief.

3. Use the first person (hence, the active voice) when a verb concerns actions by an author [investigator], "especially in matters of experimental design:" "To eliminate this possibility, I did the following experiment." Constant use of the first person, however, is distracting to a reader.

Active voice adds vitality.   Notice the vitality that results when a writer is skilled in use of the active voice. Whaley and Malott (1971) here described imprinting in chicks:

> I removed the animal from the light-proof transportation box and placed him in the center of a large four-by-ten-foot table with a one-foot-high cardboard wall around the perimeter. The 30 students in the class immediately crowded around the table to watch. In spite of my firm insistence that they maintain absolute silence, the students were unable to do so. It was quite obvious that the noise they created and the 30 eager faces peering at the chick over the cardboard railing would ruin the experiment. Nonetheless, I proceeded with the futile demonstration. I took an empty beer bottle, tied it to one end of a string, and attached the string to a pole. Then I dangled the beer bottle in front of the chick, which after a few seconds began to approach the bottle. As the bottle moved around in the enclosed space, the chick rapidly followed close behind; no matter where the bottle moved, the chick was right there. The students were amazed, but not nearly so much as I. (p. 314)

American Psychological Association recommendations.   In the third edition of the *Publication Manual of the American Psychological Association* (1983), the view is expressed that excessive use of the passive voice may lead to misplaced modifiers (p. 39) and, in the second edition (1974), that "an experienced writer can use the first person and the active voice without dominating the communication and without sacrificing the objectivity of the research" (p. 28). Some people remain skeptical. They believe that use of the first person in research reports gives too much attention to an actor. I believe the *APA Publication Manual* is correct.

Do not create inanimate (surrogate) actors.   Surrogate actors, as substitutes for a real actor, are usually inanimate objects. To make a sentence active but hide the true actor, some writers use, "This study found" rather than "The investigator found" or "Smith found." Similar substitutions include: "The theory argues" instead of "The theorist argued," or "The writing claims" instead of "Smith claims." In each of these substitutions, a *human* actor is responsible for the action; no purpose is served by giving life to an inanimate object. There are, however, some inanimate actors that must be recognized, as in "The automobile struck the post."

Similarly, in research writing, using some inanimate actors saves words, as in, "Table 1 shows that . . ." or "The data demonstrate *X*." Notice that the latter expression can be made passive by saying, "*X* is demonstrated by the data." You must judge when the savings in words is worth using the inanimate surrogate. Make minimal use of inanimate actors.

CREATING AN HONEST IMAGE

An unpretentious and nonacademic writing style puts the emphasis on *what* you have to say, not *how* you say it. Should your writing appear technical and sophisticated to make a good impression? Students often imitate erudite-sounding expressions without realizing how these damage their thinking and writing.

Here is one final suggestion: Before you begin writing your thesis, read Chapter 2, on a writer's persona, in Becker's (1986) book *Writing for Social Scientists*. That brief chapter is about creating an image. You will like the way it is written, and it may change the way you write.

References

American Chemical Society. (1986). *The ACS style guide: A manual for authors and editors*. Washington, DC: Author.

American Institute of Physics. (1978). *Style manual for the publication of papers for journals published by the American Institute of Physics and its member societies* (3rd ed., rev.). New York: Author.

American Medical Association. (1976). *Stylebook/editorial manual of the AMA* (6th ed.). Acton, MA: Publishing Sciences Group.

American National Standards Institute. (1979). *American National Standard for the preparation of scientific papers for written or oral presentation*. New York: Author.

American Psychological Association. (1974). *Publication manual of the American Psychological Association* (2nd ed.). Washington, DC: Author.

American Psychological Association. (1983). *Publication manual of the American Psychological Association* (3rd ed.). Washington, DC: Author.

American Society of Agronomy. (1984). *Publications handbook and style manual*. Madison, WI: American Society of Agronomy; Crop Science Society of America; Soil Science Society of America.

Andrews, F. M., Klem, L., Davidson, T. N., O'Malley, M. O., & Rodgers, W. L. (1975). *A guide for selecting statistical techniques for analyzing social science data*. Research monograph. Ann Arbor, MI: University of Michigan, Institute for Social Research.

Baker, S. (1976). *The complete stylist and handbook*. New York: Thomas Y. Crowell.

Becker, H. S. (1986). *Writing for social scientists*. Chicago: University of Chicago Press.

Burger on prison reform (editorial). (1981). *San Francisco Chronicle,* December 19, p. 28.

Buro's Institute of Mental Measurements. (updated volumes). *Buro's Mental Measurements Yearbooks*. Lincoln, NB: University of Nebraska Press.

CBE Style Manual Committee. (1983). *CBE style manual* (5th ed., rev.). Bethesda, MD: Author.

Christie, A. (1956). *Spider's web: a play in three acts*. London: Samuel French.

Cook, T. D., & Campbell, D. T. (1979(. *Quasi-experimentation, design and analysis issues for field settings*. Chicago: Rand McNally.

Council of Biology Editors. (1978). *Style manual* (4th ed.). Arlington, VA: Author.

Dale, E. (1953). The art of confusion. *The News Letter,* Vol. 14, No. 3. Columbus: Educational Research, Ohio State University.

English, H. B., & English, A. C. (1958). *A comprehensive dictionary of psychological and psychoanalytical terms*. New York: Longmans, Green.

Fienberg, S. E. (1980). *The analysis of cross-classified categorical data*. Boston: Massachusetts Institute of Technology Press.

Harlow, H. F. (1962). Fundamental principles for preparing psychology journal articles. *Journal of Comparative and Physiological Psychology, 55,* 893–896.

Harlow, H. F. (1971). *Learning to love*. San Francisco: Albion Publishing Company.

Kant, I. (1965). *Critique of pure reason* (Edited

and translated by N. K. Smith). New York: St. Martin's Press.

Kaplan, A. (1964). *The conduct of inquiry.* San Francisco: Chandler.

Keppel, G. (1982). *Design and analysis: A researcher's handbook.* (2nd ed.). Englewood Cliffs, NJ: Prentice-Hall, Inc.

Kirk, R. E. (1982). *Experimental design: Procedures for the behavioral sciences.* (2nd ed.). Belmont, CA: Wadsworth.

Landers, A. [newspaper column]. (1977). *The Phoenix (Arizona) Gazette,* September 14.

Laudan, L. (1977). *Progress and its problems: Toward a theory of scientific growth.* Berkeley: University of California Press.

Leggett, G., Mead, C. D., & Charvat, W. (1974). *Prentice Hall handbook for writers* (6th ed.). Englewood Cliffs, NJ: Prentice Hall.

McCrimmon, J. M. (1976). *Writing with a purpose* (6th ed.). Boston: Houghton Mifflin.

Menzel, D. H., Jones, H. M., & Boyd, L. G. (1961). *Writing a technical paper.* New York: McGraw-Hill.

Minium, E. (1978). *Statistical reasoning in psychology and education.* New York: Wiley.

Mosteller, F. 1., & Tukey, J. W. (1977). *Data analysis and regression: A second course in statistics.* Reading, MA: Addison-Wesley.

National Education Association of the United States. (1966). *NEA style manual.* Washington, DC: Author.

Pedhazur, E. J. (1982). *Multiple regression in behavioral research* (2nd ed.). New York: Holt, Rinehart and Winston.

Reiss, A. J., Jr. (1980). Victim proneness by type of crime in repeat victimization. In S. E. Fienberg & A. J. Reiss, Jr. (Eds.), *Indicators of crime and criminal justice: Quantitative studies.* Washington, DC: U.S. Government Printing Office.

Reitman, W. R. (1964). Heuristic decision procedures, open constraints, and the structure of ill-defined problems. In M. W. Shelley & G. L. Bryan (Eds.), *Human judgments and optimality.* New York: Wiley.

Russac, R. J. (1978). The relation between two strategies of cardinal number: Correspondence and counting. *Child Development, 49,* 728–735.

Shank, R., & Abelson, R. (1977). *Scripts, plans, goals and understanding.* Hillsdale, NJ: Lawrence Erlbaum Associates.

Shavelson, R. J. (1988). *Statistical reasoning for the behavioral sciences* (2nd ed.). Boston: Allyn and Bacon.

Sidman, M. (1960). *Tactics of scientific research.* New York: Basic Books.

Simon, H. A. (1973). The structure of ill structured problems. *Artificial Intelligence, 4,* 18–201.

Stock, W. A., & Dodenhoff, J. T. (1982). Characteristics of research variables and choice of statistical analyses. *Center on Evaluation, Development and Research Quarterly, 15,* 9–13.

Strunk, W., Jr., & White, W. B. (1979). *The elements of style* (3rd ed.). New York: Macmillan.

Thorndike, E. L. (1913). *Educational psychology,* Vol. 1: *The original nature of man.* New York: Teachers College, Columbia University.

Tukey, J. W. (1977). *Exploratory data analysis.* Reading, MA: Addison-Wesley.

Uhl, N. P. (1972). *The statistical interface systems,* Vol. 1: *Design selection guide.* Durham, NC: National Laboratory for Higher Education.

van Dijk, T. A., & Kintsch, W. (1983). *Strategies of discourse comprehension.* New York: Academic Press.

Vanserg, N. (1952). How to write geologese. *Economic Geology, 47*(2), 220.

Whaley, D. L., & Malott, R. (1971). *Elementary principles of behavior.* New York: Appleton-Century-Crofts.

Winer, B. J. (1979). *Statistical principles in experimental design.* New York: McGraw-Hill.

Woodford, F. P. (1967). Sounder thinking through clearer writing, *Science, 156,* 743–745.

Index